Puppets, Language and Learning

Introduction

The aim of this book is to give all adults who are involved in helping young children to learn, an insight into how and why puppets can be such powerful tools in a wide range of learning environments. Some practitioners have puppets that only appear in the classroom at circle time, and then return to the cupboard for another week — this book aims to get those puppets out of the closet and actively engaged in children's daily learning! While many of the ideas are based on learning in a nursery school setting, they can be adapted and used in the home by parents keen to share the joy of learning with their child.

Armed with only a puppet and a little imagination we can spark a child's curiousity, encourage them to believe and make believe, to dream and to enjoy the experience of learning. As adults we must appreciate that children now live in a society where they are surrounded by lively and exciting entertainment, and so to capture their imagination we need to provide them with visual, auditory and kinesthetic learning experiences which are every bit as stimulating as the latest television programmes and computer games. Puppets help us with this challenge. By introducing a new, exciting and playful character into their world, we can create a motivating and inspiring atmosphere where children enjoy learning.

Why?

Because believe me, it works! It's easy, it's fun and it does engage children in their learning. If you've ever watched a group of children sat in front of a puppet theatre or a single puppet, they are mesmerized, focused, listening, and above all happily engaged.

Who?

Who should use the puppets? If you only have one puppet, I would reserve it solely for the adult to operate. I think it's a good idea for the main teaching puppet to be seen as belonging to the teacher. The puppet has a responsible role to play in the class and is there to help with the teaching and learning. He can be used as a reward for children who are being very good and they can look after him carefully, but I would avoid this puppet venturing into the workshop or other play areas without supervision!

All adults can use puppets. Head teachers or school secretaries can have them in their offices. They can be the givers of praise and rewards, or they can be the third party listening and arbitrating between two sides of an argument. Everyone, when they appreciate the power of puppets, can use one for anything from a whole school assembly to working one to one with an individual child.

Children also love playing with puppets and they are fantastic for them to interact with, so whenever possible it's good to have some puppets that the children can use themselves. For instance, invite the children to work alongside a puppet at the writing table, share books with them in the reading corner, create meals for them, nurse them when they are poorly and play with them in role-play areas.

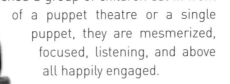

Puppets help children to empathise with other groups in society.

When?

This books aims to show that puppets can be used to enhance learning throughout the curriculum, so the simple answer to 'when?' is 'when it feels like a good idea'.

Where?

Anywhere! Puppets can be used in role-play areas, in small nurture groups, in whole class circle times, inside, outdoors and across all areas of the curriculum. There really are no limits.

What?

What or which puppets would I recommend? As a true lover and collector of puppets I am now lucky to have a cupboard stocked with a huge array and vast variety of puppets. From tiny knitted finger puppets bought at a flea market in Amsterdam, to a wonderful set of dragon puppets, complete with a dragon egg, given to me as a wedding present.

There is an endless range of puppets available to use in the classroom – from the simplest of puppets that children can make from socks and brown paper bags, to animals of all breeds and sizes and people of all races and ages. There are small finger puppets, including farm and zoo animals, birds and characters such as a witch, snowman or Santa. (Please note that for convenience we have referred to the puppets in the masculine form throughout this book).

There are many glove-sized puppets including animals such as rabbits, spiders, frogs, bears, owls, birds and hedgehogs. Then there are larger puppets, where the puppeteer's arm is used to make the mouth move, such as larger dogs or birds, and of course the various people or persona puppets which include white, Asian, and Afro-Caribbean girls and boys and Grandma and Grandpa.

How do you choose from this great array of puppets just waiting to enter your classroom? Each has a vast amount of tricks and games to play.

Different puppets can be used to inspire the varied personalities of children, and to perform different functions. A brief selection of puppets that would be useful for language development would include the following:

- **Persona puppets:** These puppets can be used either by children or adults and create a new character to interact with or build stories around.

- **Character puppets:** The Gingerbread Man, trolls, Goldilocks, Little Red Riding Hood, Jack and many more story characters, all help to bring stories to life and encourage storytelling and retelling, role-play, and inspire creative writing.

- **Animal and bird glove puppets:** From dogs to dinosaurs, and tigers to toads, there are animal puppets to inspire every child to speak, listen, read and write.

- **Finger puppets:** Easy to handle, finger puppets of every imaginable description can be used to recreate scenarios or create imaginary stories, and to play a host of language games.

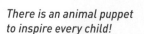

There is an animal puppet to inspire every child!

How to choose your first puppet

- **Make the puppet special for you:** If you are in a fabulous toy shop and spot a puppet that really takes your fancy – then that's the one. If you visit an Educational Show and see one that inspires you, buy it! If you surf the online puppet suppliers and see something that stops you in your tracks – then that's your puppet! The ethos behind using puppets is all about enjoyment and active learning – if you love 'him', then so will they.

- **Make the puppet special for your audience:** If you know that a child you are struggling to engage has a real interest in football, choose a boy puppet and give him a football badge, or make him a small stripy scarf in the local team's colours.

- **Size doesn't matter:** (but cost might!) The best puppet for you is not necessarily the biggest. Especially when you are beginning to use puppets you may find the larger ones a bit more daunting to handle. Although many of the activities in the book have been written as if for a large persona puppet, they can all be adapted for a simple finger puppet. I keep attached to my bag a small dragon puppet and I call him my 'magic dragon'. On visits to other classes or schools he often leaves my bag and has an impromptu learning experience with some children. I also have a tiny mouse finger puppet in my collection and he has been involved in some fabulous story writing, when the children pretend that he's actually someone who has been turned into a mouse by a wicked witch.

- **DIY puppets:** (when cost really does matter!) Puppets are fun to make, and as well as designing your own puppets, you can make simple puppets with the children. A sock can be turned into a glove puppet, or the fingers from gloves decorated to make finger puppets. Felt has the advantage of not fraying and can be cut and stitched easily to create basic puppets. Soft toys can be converted into puppets by undoing a seam and removing some of the filling. Some items such as oven gloves or sponge mitts can also be turned into very effective puppets. For more ideas on making your own puppets go to Techniques and tips page 57.

- **Share!** My colleagues know the inhabitants of my cupboard and come and borrow puppets on a regular basis. Similarly, if they purchase new ones, they come and show off their new acquisitions to me, and we share resources. When your class moves to a new year group a puppet can be used to help with the transition. It can be effective to let their new teacher borrow a favourite puppet for a few weeks, and then invite your old class back to talk about all that they have learnt — passing messages back to you via the puppet about what they now know.

- **One is never enough!** Once you have experienced the magic that puppets can evoke in the classroom you will no doubt wish to expand your collection. At this point it is worth thinking about any particular stories or topics that the children are going to cover through the school year and try to find puppets that will fit in with them. For instance, there are some versatile puppets available including one wonderful rabbit hidden inside a lettuce. Under the leaves there is a whole collection of minibeast finger puppets. The finger puppets can be used individually and the rabbit in the lettuce can hide all kinds of other props in the leaves such as different food, letter cards or measuring worms.

Puppets can be placed in any setting you choose.

- **All singing and dancing:** It may be worth considering what you would like the puppet to be able to do. Does it need to make a noise? Sometimes it is good to have a puppet that squeaks as though it is talking, although if the noise is simply to gain the children's attention, or if they are counting the number of times they hear a sound, then you could just use it to hold a percussion instrument. Do you need the puppet to be able to hold things or to sit on your knee? Remember though that a puppet can have its own special bag, box or suitcase for props and that way it can introduce things to the class without having to be able to hold them.

Puppets and children

From their earliest years children relate to puppets because they are used to making inanimate objects come to life. Children themselves are puppeteers from the first time they pick up a shoe, a squeezed out half orange, or a hairbrush and make it move or talk. Toys and dolls have an active role in children's play. They laugh, talk and argue. They 'try on' personalities and 'take them off' again. The child makes her doll move – she is the puppeteer. She scolds her doll in a stern but loving voice like a parent – she is the actor. She makes her doll stamp its foot and then laughs at the effect – she is the audience. After this early experience of play, a child recognises puppets as both legitimate and natural.

The puppet can be whatever the puppeteer and child make him. He can be the child's friend without demanding something in return. He can be a funny clown to make them laugh. He can be naughty and get into trouble without hurting anyone. He can say what the child thinks and feel what the child feels and share a child's sadness. He can show a child who knows poverty, hunger, war and loss that there can also be joy and love and a happy ending. A puppet can tell a child who rarely hears it that he is loved. A puppet can show a child that her mother or father can also be sad, and he can demonstrate the value of love, the futility of quarrels and the benefit of co-operation and support.

The work of Unicef [1] provides some powerful examples of how puppets can be used to involve children. They have projects in Indonesia where puppets are used to teach children the importance of hygiene and hand washing. Through puppet stories and songs, the children learn lessons that could ultimately save their lives. They then learn to perform their own stories and songs and promote the message to their school friends.

There are further examples of puppets being used to welcome children back to school in Pakistan after the Tsunami. Here puppet shows are not just fun and games. They provide psychological support and contain useful messages about daily life, such as good hygiene practices. In Grenada, Unicef runs a programme called the 'Return to Happiness' project for children affected by Hurricane 'Ivan'. Using a family of rag doll puppets, and stories and songs they aim to help these children overcome their personal pain.

Their worker says:

> 'the use of puppets can allow the children to express their feelings more easily and openly than if they were speaking by themselves.' [1]

The puppet can be whatever the puppeteer and the child make him.

Puppets and learning

Life and learning for children should be full of fun and enjoyment so it needs to be play-based and something that they want to be actively engaged in. Recent research on the brain tells us that learning is most successful when children find it fun. If children establish a belief that learning is hard, difficult, boring, or simply that they are poor at it, they may carry this belief with them through out their school days, and will not reach their full potential. Negative attitudes towards learning can be changed, but it is much better to ensure that children find learning exciting and fun from the start. Research also shows that fifty per cent of a person's ability to learn is developed in the first four years of life, and another thirty percent is developed by the time a child is eight! This does not mean that children absorb half their knowledge by the time they are four, but that half the main learning pathways in their brains are developed during those formative years.

Brains are fully engaged in their learning when we can see happy, smiling faces and hear the sounds of giggles and gasps of excitement.

'We discovered that education is not something which the teacher does, but that it is a natural process which develops spontaneously in the human being. It is not acquired by listening to words, but in virtue of experiences in which the child acts on his environment. The teacher's task is not to talk, but to prepare and arrange a series of motives for cultural activity in a special environment made for the child.'

Dr. Maria Montessori

'80 percent of learning difficulties are related to stress. Remove the stress and you remove the difficulties.'

(Gordon Stokes 'One brain: Dyslexic learning correction and brain integration.'[2])

Puppets are the tools that we can use to let the children feel that they are being entertained as well as taught. We only need a little imagination to see in how many different ways we can use puppets in our teaching and their learning.

To ensure that children learn effectively we need to engage, motivate and inspire them. Canadian teachers, Anne Forester and Margaret Reinhard in their book, 'The Learner's Way' [3], talk of 'creating a climate of delight' in every classroom. They consider variety, surprise, imagination and challenge are essential in creating that climate. Using puppets helps to foster this 'climate of delight.' Colourful and interesting puppets, using a variety of inspiring props, will stimulate those who are mainly 'visual learners'. Adding sound to sessions by welcoming children with a puppet singing a song, or using percussion instruments will stimulate the 'auditory learners'. 'Kinesthetic learners' need practitioners to be exciting, creative and practical; they need to know that there will be plenty of 'fun' activities for them to do.

Finger puppets help to create a 'climate of delight' for children.

Children learn experientially through getting visually, aurally and kinaesthetically involved in a subject. Puppets are bright and colourful, tactile and moving. They engage the child as a whole person, bringing in several of Gardener's multiple intelligences especially emotional, spatial, interpersonal and intrapersonal [4]. This increases the childrens' interest in the lesson and leads to a deeper level of learning.

Eric Jensen, author of 'Super Teaching' [5], believes that there are three core elements that effect learning. The first two are 'state' and 'strategy'. State creates the right mood for learning, and using a puppet in the classroom undoubtedly helps create that positive 'mood'. Strategy denotes the style or method of presentation and again puppets enable practitioners to use a range of strategies to ensure that all learners are involved. The third element is 'content', and to keep the content inspirational and exciting, it's important that children find it fun and this is easily achievable when using a puppet. It's also important that children see a relevance to what they are learning and so by being able to set up real scenarios around the puppet, children can see that number and language skills are used in many areas of our everyday lives.

While many of the activities suggested in this book could be done without the aid of a puppet, by using puppets children are more engaged and are likely to be increasingly motivated and show better concentration. There is something about using a puppet that turns a lesson into a more interactive experience, more like a 'show', within which the audience is expected and invited to become actively involved.

The puppet can be used in different roles in the various activities so that it does not always take on the lead role, and children will enjoy having their turn at entertaining and teaching the puppet too. Swapping the roles between pupils, puppets and practitioners illustrates to the children that we all learn in different ways. Often children learn best when they are encouraged to explain how they found an answer, and in doing so they are cementing that knowledge in their own brain, while also gaining in self esteem with that wondrous feeling of 'I can do it now' or even 'I can help you do it too!'

Puppets love fun!
Here the puppet enjoys
a ride at the zoo.

Puppets in the EYFS

Children's first experiences at school are crucial to their future success and can help to build a secure foundation for their learning throughout their school years and beyond. The key to achieving a positive early experience of learning is to try to make it as enjoyable and memorable as possible.

Children will enter settings with a range of individual needs, interests and at different stages of development and so planning and delivering a relevant and enjoyable curriculum across all the areas of learning can pose practitioners with quite a challenge. Using puppets helps to add elements of fun, drama, excitement, and interaction to the children's experience of learning.

Puppets are also a useful way of ensuring that the six 'Areas of Learning and Development' covered by the EYFS can be presented in a more integrated or cross-curricular style – as the class puppet or character can work in different areas, bringing with it skills and knowledge and modelling how they can be applied in different contexts. The balance between purposeful play, adult-led and child-initiated activities can also be supported through the use of puppets.

> 'Children must be provided with experiences and support which will help them to develop a positive sense of themselves and of others: respect for others; social skills; and a positive disposition to learn. Providers must ensure support for children's emotional wellbeing to help them to know themselves and what they can do'
>
> Statutory Framework for the Early Years Foundation Stage (2008)

Personal, social and emotional development

Puppets can be used to aid communication and team work.

Playing with puppets can have a very positive impact on a young child's personal, social and emotional development. The following ideas and activities are linked to the appropriate early learning goals.

Form good relationships with adults and peers/work as part of a group or class, taking turns and sharing fairly, understanding that there needs to be agreed values and codes of behaviour for groups of people, including adults and children, to work together harmoniously.
A child that has not yet developed the skill of playing with other children can begin by playing with a puppet. The child will be practising and learning how to interact and have dialogue with another person, while they are chatting to their puppet. A child who is not happy taking turns or sharing, may find it easier or less threatening if they start by giving the puppet a turn. In this situation they can feel more confident because they know that they are in control — they will get their turn next as the puppet is not going to refuse to give the toy back! Through this role–play the child begins to feel more comfortable playing with others.

Have a developing awareness of their own needs, views and feelings and be sensitive to the needs, views and feelings of others/consider the consequences of their words and actions for themselves and others.

A puppet is never going to pass judgement on a child — they are safe to be themselves, to share their secrets and their feelings, and know that the puppet is never going to mock or laugh at them, unless of course they choose to make the puppet naughty or unkind in their play. Even a rude, badly behaved puppet can not do the damage and cause the upset that a child or adult would because the children all know that the puppet is 'only pretending'.

> 'Sam (the puppet) is really sad because ...
> Can anyone think what we could do to cheer him up?

Respond to significant experiences, showing a range of feelings when appropriate .

Try using puppets to talk to the children about situations or incidents without mentioning any of the children's names. By talking through a third party the children are often more likely to share their views and express how they feel.

In the magical world of puppets, the bird and zebra can become friends

Have a developing respect for their own cultures and beliefs and those of other people/understand that they can expect others to treat their needs, views, cultures and beliefs with respect.

The availability of puppets of varied races and ages is an effective way to encourage the children to think and talk about their own views, religions, homes and families. The Asian girl puppet, Farzana, sparked off much discussion among the children about their own visits to Pakistan. They talked about her clothing, admiring it, but commenting on the fact that she had no bracelets (something I am sure they will enjoy remedying). They enjoyed the fact that the puppet was not yet able to speak English, and so talked with the aid of a bi-lingual assistant. The children taught Farzana to count in Punjabi and English, and at circle time they asked if they could say goodbye to her in Punjabi. She went round the circle with many of the children choosing to say goodbye to her in their first language and then giving her a hug.

Have a developing awareness of their own needs, views and feelings and be sensitive to the needs, views and feelings of others.

Keep a special puppet out of sight one day and wait for the children to start asking about her. What could be wrong with her? Who might be caring for her? Has she been to visit the doctor? Who would help her take her medicine? All the time the children are drawing on their own knowledge and experience, and then extending it in a way which is meaningful to them.

Puppets can be used to get children talking and thinking about their own personal health. Caring about a puppet can develop into caring about each other.

Puppets can feel lonely too!

Playing with animal puppets encourages children to consider how they would take care of a real pet. The school environment and the rigors of health and safety regulations might not make it feasible to keep a real dog or a rabbit as a pet in school but a puppet pet would still need a home, a basket, food and would most certainly need playing with in a kind and sensitive way. The puppet pet could even go home each weekend with a different child, who could then tell the class all about what they got up to on Monday morning. Put together a book to accompany the pet home including care instructions, a disposable camera and blank paper for the child to record what the pet did in their home.

Dress and undress independently and manage their own personal hygiene

Talk to the children about the clothes that the puppet is wearing. Is she appropriately dressed for today's weather? What would happen if she played outside without a coat in the winter? Sun safety can also be discussed in a way which the children will remember. Encourage them to talk about keeping safe in the sun and listen to the reasons why it is important to protect themselves — the auditory learners will remember this. Then dress the puppet in an outrageous sunhat and some trendy sunglasses and pretend to rub some sun cream on her — the visual learners will remember this sight. Any kinaesthetic learners will now want to run outside with the puppet and play — and will hopefully remember to put their own sunhats on.

> *'Children's learning and competence in communicating, speaking and listening, being read to and beginning to read and write must be supported and extended. They must be provided with opportunity and encouragement to use their skills in a range of situations and for a range of purposes, and be supported in developing the confidence and disposition to do so.'*
>
> Statutory Framework for the Early Years Foundation Stage (2008)

Puppets can be used to encourage turn taking and sharing.

Communication, language and literacy

Using puppets to encourage communication

Interact with others, negotiating plans and activities and taking turns in conversation.
Communication skills can be modelled through puppets in a variety of ways. Simply holding a small puppet with his head turned away or down, will entice a child to ask, 'What's wrong?' How do they know something is wrong with the puppet? A discussion can follow about the puppet's body language, what we could do to find out what's wrong, and what to do next. Puppets are an ideal way of demonstrating non-verbal communication, for instance, if a puppet points at something, the child may ask several questions. 'Why is he doing that?' 'Does he want this?' 'Does he want to go over there?' In talking this through with the child, we demonstrate that we can communicate some things through gestures, but that words make our messages much clearer.

Enjoy listening to and using spoken and written language, and readily turn to it in their play and learning/use language to imagine and recreate roles and experiences.
Young children enjoy taking puppets into the home corner or other role-play areas. They can make him something to eat, or look after the puppet when he's feeling poorly, and they can play endless games with their 'friend'.

Puppets can be used to teach children to care for others.

The puppet is a constant listener and allows the child time to practise and rehearse what they want to say. Puppets encourage children to ask questions and share their own opinions. Often if a puppet has asked the question, then the children may be less concerned about whether their answer is right and they will feel more confident about sharing their views. The puppet is free to express his opinions — he can whisper that he doesn't like a particular book. Children feel free to agree or disagree with a puppet, while sometimes they might feel obliged to agree with their teacher, thinking that seems the 'right' thing to do.

Reading with puppets

Listen with enjoyment and respond to stories, songs and other music, rhymes and poems and make up their own stories, songs, rhymes and poems/retell narratives in the correct sequence, drawing on language patterns of stories.
A puppet can visit your setting and bring with him a favourite book that he wants to share with the children. He can sit on the practitioner's knee and help turn the pages and show the children that he is listening carefully to the story by looking at the storyteller. The puppet can glance round at the children and whisper in the reader's ear the names of any children who are listening really well. No doubt as soon as the puppet has spotted one child sitting and appearing to be riveted by the story, then suddenly there will be lots of children keen to show him that they too are really interested in the story. How much more curiosity will the children show in the story when they know it's the puppet's favourite? Perhaps it was the puppet's birthday present or a new picture book he bought on holiday. The puppet can encourage the children to bring in their favourite books to share with him too.

Know that print carries meaning and, in English, is read from left to right and top to bottom/ show an understanding of the elements of stories, such as main character, sequence of events, and openings.

Puppets can be used as props for storytelling. A bear puppet might be used to bring all sorts of stories about bears to life, and can then tell the practitioner some extra background details about the characters and their adventures that aren't in the book. The bear knows what happened next, but can the children guess? Children can 'read' their book or tell their story to the puppet — they will have a captive audience that will respond in whatever way they choose, and will certainly not criticise them.

Ben's Diary

Written by Reception Yellow & Miss Fisher
Illustrated by Reception Yellow & Miss Fisher.
Hovingham Primary .Leeds. 2003

Writing with puppets

Attempt writing for different purposes, using features of different forms such as lists, stories and instructions. All puppets have birthdays, and some celebrate different festivals such as Christmas, Eid, Divali or Chinese New Year. These all provide lots of different opportunities for children to write. The puppets all need cards making for them and letters writing to them. They want invitations to parties, shopping lists and appointment cards. They may want to reply, but they will need some help when trying to write back, and who better to help them do that than their friends — the children? Perhaps the puppet could keep a diary, and the children could help suggest what he might like to put in it each day.

Write their own names and other things such as labels and captions, and begin to form sentences, sometimes using punctuation/use a pencil and hold it effectively to form recognisable letters, most of which are correctly formed.

Puppets can be very keen to form their letters correctly and to learn how to write their names. They can visit the setting with some very special pens, pencils and paper, and be happy to share these with the children. Some of the large persona puppets have hands that fit like gloves and so the practitioner can actually make the puppet write. With lots of practice these puppets can even have a go at playing the keyboard and using the computer! Alternatively, try using a small finger puppet on the end of a whiteboard pen to comment on the moves as the practitioner models letter formation. What happens when letters are not correctly formed? Can the children help the puppet to do better?

This puppet is learning to write her name!

Problem solving, reasoning and numeracy

> 'Children must be supported in developing their understanding of Problem Solving, Reasoning and Numeracy in a broad range of contexts in which they can explore, enjoy, learn, practise and talk about their developing understanding. They must be provided with opportunities to practise and extend their skills in these areas to gain confidence and competence in their use.'
>
> Statutory Framework for the Early Years Foundation Stage (2008)

Say and use number names in order in familiar contexts/count reliably up to ten everyday objects/ recognise numerals one to nine.

Puppets can help bring a wide range of number songs and rhymes to life. How much more fun it is to sing "Five little ducks went swimming" when five children can come out and use finger puppets of ducklings. "Five little speckled frogs" is much more fun when you involve frog finger puppets. Special puppet gloves are available to buy with a little duck, monkey, frog or spaceman at the end of each finger to accompany different number rhymes. Children will enjoy designing their own puppet gloves and making up songs to go with them.

A game to play

The little speckled frog has a great mum who turns up to help her little frogs learn to count. She shows them lily pads with numbers on and the little frogs have to learn how to jump across them in the right order. Mum can tease them by sitting on a lily pad and they have to guess which number she is hiding. Once the children have seen the games the frogs can play, they can be given a box with the finger puppets, plastic frogs and lily pads for them to make up their own games.

The glove puppet with a frog on each finger helps the children visualise what is happening in the story.

Count reliably up to ten everyday objects/recognise numerals one to nine/find one more or one less than a number from one to ten.

The gingerbread man puppet can stride up and down a number line. The children can predict which number he will be on when he makes one more step forward, or takes one step backwards. The gingerbread man can kick a ball to and fro with another puppet while the children count how many times they can kick the ball. The children could estimate how many times the puppets are going to be able to kick the ball, or they could keep a tally to help them count.

Count reliably up to ten everyday objects/recognise numerals one to nine/use language such as 'more' or 'less' to compare two numbers.

Puppets that make a noise are great fun for helping children to count. The children can pick a number card and show it to the puppet who then tries to squawk or make a noise the correct number of times. If he gets it right the children give him a thumbs up, but if he gets it wrong he gets a thumbs down and the children have to come and help. They can clap the right number for the puppet and show him the correct number of fingers. The puppet might still get it wrong. Has the puppet counted too many or too few?

Some large bird puppets can even hold a pen in their beaks and have a go at writing numbers with the children. Even a tiny finger puppet can get involved in counting – he can nod or bow the correct number of times and as he grows in confidence he will get quicker. Can the children keep up with him?

Count reliably up to ten everyday objects/use developing mathematical ideas and methods to solve practical problems.

Larger character puppets can visit the children with number cards, marbles, beads or coins in their pockets or bags. They can show children their coins and then pretend to lose one or tease them by hiding one. Which coin is missing? Let the children play with a puppet and encourage them to devise their own games to play with the puppet to help it learn to count.

Use language such as 'greater', 'smaller', 'heavier' or 'lighter' to compare quantities/talk about, recognise and recreate simple patterns.

Puppets need all sorts of things making for them. A girl puppet might need a new necklace. Show the children some different lengths of string and let them choose which one they think would be the best to use? Which one is going to be too short and which is too long? The puppet can tell the children which shape or colour is her favourite and the children can sort through the beads to find the puppet's favourites. The puppet might show the children a pattern that she likes and then the children could use it to make the necklace.

Use language such as 'circle' or 'bigger' to describe the shape and size of solid and flat shapes.

Show the children a tray full of shapes and then play 'Kim's game'. A naughty puppet comes along and hides one of the shapes. Can the children tell which one is missing or ask the puppet for a few clues to help. 'The shape hidden in my pocket looks like the shape of the clock on the wall'. When the children guess right, they can take turns to hide the shape away from the puppet and get him to guess. Can they think of new clues to help. All the time the children will think they are playing games and having fun with a character they like. They will remember how they laughed when 'Grandma' tucked the triangle up her jumper, or the frog nearly choked on a square!

Knowledge and understanding of the world

> *'Children must be supported in developing the knowledge, skills and understanding that help them to make sense of the world. Their learning must be supported through offering opportunities for them to use a range of tools safely; encounter creatures, people, plants, and objects in their natural environments and in real-life situations; undertake practical 'experiments'; and work with a range of materials.'*
>
> **Statutory Framework for the Early Years Foundation Stage (2008)**

In early year's settings it is best to think of this goal as 'Knowledge and understanding of *their* world'.

Investigate objects and materials by using all their senses as appropriate/ask questions about why things happen and how things work.

The puppet can bring in some flowers from the garden to show to the children. Together they can arrange the flowers in a vase. The puppet will of course need reminding to put water in the vase and the children can explain why. When the puppet asks 'Why do the flowers need water?' the children know that the teacher already has the right answer. The puppet however, doesn't know and this gives the child permission to think about the question and answer it with out any fear of being wrong. If the answer is wrong the puppet can always say 'Hmmm, I wonder, I thought maybe it was because.... What do you think?' When children learn in this way their brains are engaged and active and so the knowledge is more likely to be retained.

Find out about, and identify, some features of living things, objects and events they observe/ observe, find out about and identify features in the place they live and the natural world.

Before going on a visit to a farm let the children look at books about farm animals and sing some songs such as 'Old McDonald had a farm'. Pack the books, a recording of the song, some plastic farm animals and a set of finger puppets of farm animals into a large shoe box and let the children play. They will discover lots about the farm and enjoy playing with the puppets. Can they make the right sounds for the different animals?

Puppets want to share their excitement and encourage us to learn about our world.

When visting the farm yourself to write a risk assessment for the trip, take the class puppet along too. Take photographs yourself of the puppet enjoying his visit, and of course staying to the path and not putting his fingers through the fence. The children will be even more excited about their forthcoming trip when they see the photos and can ask the puppet all kinds of questions about the farm. Alternatively, purchase a souvenir from the gift shop and give it to the puppet. The children will be curious to know how the puppet got the badge or pen.

Ask questions about why things happen and how things work/find out about past and present events in their own lives, and those of their families and other people they know.
Character puppets can spark off all kind of discussions and investigations. The bus ticket in the pocket – 'Where have you come from?' and 'When are you going back?' The receipt in the pocket – 'Where have you been shopping and what did you buy?' The photograph in the pocket – 'Who is that?' and 'Where are you now?' The letter in the pocket – 'Who is it from and what is their news?' Props like these encourage the children to talk about places they have been, people who they know and events that they have experienced.

Investigate objects and materials by using all of their senses as appropriate/find out about their environment, and talk about those features they like and dislike.
The puppet can come to school without a coat. The children will have to decide if it's warm enough for the puppet to go outside to play without a coat. The weather gets warmer and the puppet wants to play out again. Now the puppet needs a sun hat and the children could help to make one. They can learn all about the weather and the different seasons by thinking about what the puppet might need in its wardrobe.

Find out about past and present events in their own lives, and those of their families and other people they know/begin to know about their own cultures and beliefs and those of other people.
Grandma and grandpa puppets can be used to encourage the children to talk about age and growing older. They can see that Grandma has got grey hair and that Grandpa doesn't have much hair at all. They can compare the way the puppets look and dress with the older people in their family. They can look at childhood photographs of the adults in the setting and see that once they were younger. Puppets can have birthdays and join in celebrations of different festivals. When is the puppet's birthday? Make a birth certificate for each puppet. What information does it tell us about them? Talk about families and find out about the puppet's family and home.

Puppets enjoy the outdoors and playing sport.

Observe, find out about and identify features in the place they live and the natural world/find out about and identify the uses of everyday technology and use information and communication technology to support their learning.

Show the children pictures of the puppets playing in the local park or sitting on the beach, and suddenly the children will realise that the puppets can be anywhere they want to be. Unleash their imagination and let them play. If you don't feel happy taking the puppets out with you, take some pictures of them and then use some photo software to cut and paste them out of one setting and into another! The possibilities are endless. Show the children how to use ICT to cut and paste pictures of their favourite puppet into different settings.

Puppets enjoy their time at school, but they too can have lots of fun on holiday!

Although possibly the most exciting place for any puppet to be is in your classroom – there are so many different characters to meet, places to be, and so much exciting learning to do.

Physical development

> 'The physical development of babies and young children must be encouraged through the provision of opportunities for them to be active and interactive and to improve their skills of co-ordination, control, manipulation and movement. They must be supported in using all their senses to learn about the world around them and to make connections between new information and what they already know. They must be supported in developing an understanding of the importance of physical activity and making healthy choices in relation to food.'
>
> Statutory Framework for the Early Years Foundation Stage (2008)

Move with confidence, imagination and in safety/move with control and coordination.
Children cannot resist moving when there is a puppet about. Within the foundation stage anything that encourages children to move, explore and touch will enhance their physical development and so getting puppets into the classroom will help. Children will be keen to come and interact or play with the puppets.

Recognise the importance of keeping healthy, and those things which contribute to this.
The puppet knows a lot about eating a good healthy diet. He can write his shopping lists with the children. Sometimes the puppet might put sweets and fizzy drinks on the lists, and then the children will have to decide if they think that's a good idea. The puppets and the children can join together in some simple aerobic or keep fit exercises.

Puppets enjoy dancing at a school disco.

Travel around, under, over and through balancing and climbing equipment.

Where a child is not yet confident about an activity such as climbing on the A-frame or going down a slide, the puppet can encourage a child to have a go. By giving the puppet instructions and praising him for doing well, the child will feel more confident, gain some self-belief and hopefully be able to try the activity themselves.

Use a range of small and large equipment/ handle tools, objects, construction and malleable materials safely and with increasing control.

The simple movement of making a puppet talk refines a child's fine motor skills and pincer movement. The children have to be able to move their fingers to either open or close the puppet's mouth sufficiently so that it looks like it's talking. Without this fine control they can end up with the puppet looking like it is always gasping in amazement. Using finger puppets and glove puppets also develops a child's ability to handle small items and gain increasing fine motor control.

Creative development

'Children's creativity must be extended by the provision of support for their curiosity, exploration and play. They must be provided with opportunities to explore and share their thoughts, ideas and feelings, for example, through a variety of art, music, movement, dance, imaginative and role-play activities, mathematics, and design and technology.'

Statutory Framework for the Early Years Foundation Stage (2008)

Explore colour, texture, shape, form and space in two or three dimensions/use their imagination in art and design, music, dance, imaginative and role–play and stories.

Puppets open up all kinds of opportunities for children to think creatively. They can draw pictures, paint portraits of puppets, or invent songs, rhymes and games to play with a puppet. The children can create plays and songs with the characters inspired by the puppets e.g. the toucan or bird puppet doesn't like the sound of its squawk and wants the children to help him make other sounds using their own voices or different musical instruments. They can write a song for him to sing. They can make up a drama about the puppet who has lost his favourite toy or act out traditional stories using different puppets.

Express and communicate their ideas, thoughts and feelings by using a widening range of materials, suitable tools, imaginative and role-play, movement, designing and making, and a variety of songs and musical instruments.

> *Children can make their own puppets to use in imaginative play. For lots of ideas on this see Making puppets on p. 57 or go to Tips and techniques on p. 53*

The children can help the puppet when he moves house and he wants some pictures to hang up in his new bedroom. He would like a portrait of his new friends and a picture of himself too. He might even need someone to plan a layout for his room. The children can use their knowledge of their own bedrooms to decide what the puppet would need in his bedroom. Can the children design some new wallpaper, curtains or bedding for the puppet? The children can use catalogues and cut out pictures to make a collage version of their 'fantasy bedroom'.

Children can have great fun designing and creating things, from a racing car for a boy or girl puppet, to a special kennel for a dog puppet. A fluffy pink dog puppet would require a rather special version of a kennel as well as a fine new collar and lead. The children can discuss what length of lead the dog might need, and so the activity generates cross-curricular discussion which enhances their creative thinking. At the same time it develops their mathamatical skills by giving them practical experience of terms such as long, longer, short, shorter, etc.

The puppet can introduce the children to new creative mediums. He could bring into school a selection of things he found at the beach, or in the park, and ask the children to help create a picture using them to remind him of a special day out. The children can use the objects to print with, or stick the pieces together to create a collage or a 3D sculpture. The puppet can suggest that the children bring in some natural objects that they have found and use them to create their own picture.

Recognise and explore how sounds can be changed, sing simple songs from memory, recognise repeated sounds and sound patterns and match movements to music.

The puppet knows a lot! Puppets can teach songs to the children and show them different ways of using their voices. The bird puppet could sing very high and the lion puppet very low to demonstrate 'pitch'. The children can echo clap rhythm patterns played by a puppet on the drum. Character puppets with different names can be used to introduce word rhythms such as Fred, Polly and Christopher.

A puppet provides an appropriate audience to any musical experience.

> *The traditional Chinese proverb says, 'I hear and I forget, I see and I hear, and I may remember, I do and I understand.'* I would add... 'I do it with a puppet, and I smile and understand. The memory of the smile helps me remember how I understood my learning.'

Teaching and learning literacy with puppets

Children, in their acquisition of language, need to develop skills in speaking, listening, reading and writing. These skills will help them to express themselves creatively and imaginatively and to communicate with others effectively. The development of these skills can be a daunting challenge to both the child and the teacher – for we all know that for every rule taught about the English language there will also be an exception to that rule! This section looks at how puppets can be used to make both teaching and learning in literacy engaging, fun and meaningful. It takes objectives from the new Literacy Framework and suggests lots of different ideas for using puppets to teach and learn together.

Speaking

Speaking and listening are the first essential building blocks in a child's language development. Until a child can speak a sentence, they cannot be expected to write a sentence. Until a child can listen to a question, they cannot answer it. It is vital that children have the confidence to express themselves and practise these skills, and by using puppets to help with the acquisition of these early language stepping stones, the adult can ensure that the child is having fun and feels secure enough to have a go.

Year 1 Learning objectives	Year 2 Learning objectives
Retell stories, ordering events using story language	Speak with clarity and use appropriate intonation when reading and reciting texts
Tell stories and describe incidents from their own experience in an audible voice	Tell real and imagined stories using the conventions of familiar story language
Interpret a text by reading aloud with some variety in pace and emphasis	Explain ideas and processes using imaginative and adventurous vocabulary and non-verbal gestures to support communication
Experiment with and build new stores of words to communicate in different contexts	

Puppet activities

- **Tell me a tale:** Telling a story or recounting an event is much more engaging when it's told to someone who knows nothing about it. Children can retell a story to the puppet that the teacher has read to them while he has been absent from school. The puppet can ask questions to make sure he (and the children) really understand the story and the sequence of events. The puppet could model trying to remember the story and jot the key events onto a story board or put ideas about characters on to a word web.

- **What's my story?** The puppet can bring in a bag with some objects in it or wear a special badge or item of clothing. Show the children what the puppet has brought in. Where could he have been? What could he have been up to? Invite the children to find out more by looking at the objects carefully and asking the puppet appropriate questions. The puppet could ask the children similar questions to find out what they have been up to.

Young children enjoy having puppets to play with. They can make the puppet something to eat, or look after him when he's feeling poorly, and they can play endless games with their 'friend'. Essentially the difference between a puppet and an ordinary soft toy is that with a soft toy a child may choose to talk to it, but a puppet actively encourages their child to interact with

it. As soon as a child puts their finger into a finger puppet or hand into a glove puppet he will realise that then he can make it move and so it will come 'alive' in his hands. This interaction between the child and the puppet is vital, as the acquisition of speaking and listening skills requires a child to understand the need to communicates with others.

Puppets and children with additional needs

Playing alongside a child or group of children with a puppet gives the adult the opportunity to model conversational language and social interaction. Children who find it hard to communicate with others can start to talk without pressure or fear of criticism. The puppet will always listen and respond in the way the child wants it to.

A puppet can be like a pet for the children to care for and play with.

Puppets understand all languages! A child can talk with their puppet in any language and will imagine the puppet is responding in that chosen language. For children who are new to English, having a puppet to play with helps them to feel less isolated when children around them are speaking a language they don't yet understand. Soon other children will want to join in and play alongside them.

The adult does not need to be a ventriloquist.
With a bit of practise it is easy for an adult to make children believe that a puppet is talking. One effective way to operate a puppet is to hold his face towards your ear and appear to be listening, while moving the puppet's mouth a little. Then tell the children what the puppet has just whispered to you.

Puppets understand all languages!

Listening and responding

Year 1 Learning objectives	Year 2 Learning objectives
Listen with sustained concentration, building new stores of words in different contexts	Listen to others in class, ask relevant questions and follow instructions
Listen to and follow instructions accurately, asking for help and clarification if necessary	Listen to talk by an adult, remember some specific points and identify what they have learned
Listen to tapes or video and express views about how a story or information has been presented	Respond to presentations by describing characters, repeating some highlights and commenting constructively

Puppet activities

- **Puppet band:** The puppet has a collection of percussion instruments. He demonstrates each to the children and names them. Now he can play an instrument and the children have to guess which one it is. Place a barrier in front of the instruments – a large book, piece of card or a screen. The puppet can then invite the child who guessed correctly to come and join the band. The puppet chooses one instrument and the child a second. Can the children name the two instruments they hear?

- **Play it again!** This is an extension of the previous activity. The puppet chooses an instrument from his collection and plays a simple rhythm – it could be the pattern of a child's name or a simple combination of long and short sounds. The children have to name the instrument and echo the rhythm. Swap over and let a child make up the rhythm for the puppet to copy.

- **Draw my picture:** The children sit on the carpet with small whiteboards and pens. The puppet has his own board and pen and sits on the teacher's knee. He does a simple drawing on his board, describing it as he draws and the children follow his instructions. He can describe putting different shapes next to, on top of, or underneath something, etc. When the drawing is finished the children show the puppet their boards and he can exclaim, 'Wow! You must have listened really carefully to get your picture to look like mine without even looking at it!' Once children are familiar with playing copying games like this, they can play together in pairs – one child giving clear instructions and the other child listening and following them. If a child is shy and needs encouragement they can be given the puppet to hold, and often this stops them feeling nervous and helps them to enjoy the game as they make the puppet play, draw and talk.

- **Puppet whispers:** Puppets can play simple games like Chinese whispers and of course be blamed when the whisper goes wrong!

A puppet will listen to all your secrets!

Puppet lists: Puppets can lead a variety of circle games. He can start with a statement such as 'I was hungry at lunchtime, so I ate a kipper!' Each child has to add another item on to the list and remember what has already been said! By the time it gets back to the puppet he can tell the children that he feels very poorly now! Also if a child gets stuck, rather than feeling nervous about not being able to continue, the puppet can say that he feels full now, and can start a new game. 'After my lunch I played football.'

- **It's my story:** Using a puppet is a wonderful way to introduce a new story or book. He can bring with him a beautifully wrapped parcel which the children will be excited to see. Choose a child to help unwrap it and to discover that it is a birthday present for the puppet and then share the book together. Alternatively, use a puppet that is the same as a character in the book, for instance, an owl puppet to share 'Owl babies' or a bear puppet to share 'Where's my Teddy?'.

Group discussion and interaction

Year 1 Learning objectives	Year 2 Learning objectives
Take turns to speak, listen to other's suggestions and talk about what they are going to do	Ensure that everyone contributes, allocate tasks, and consider alternatives and reach agreement
Ask and answer questions, make relevant contributions, offer suggestions and take turns	Work effectively in groups by ensuring that each group member takes a turn challenging, supporting and moving on
Explain their views to others in a small group; decide how to report the group's views to the class	Listen to each other's views and preferences, agree the next steps to take and identify contributions by each group member

Puppet activities:

- **Group dynamics:** For some children the first obstacle to working collaboratively as a group is that more than one child may want to be in charge. If each group can have a puppet as team leader it solves this problem! The puppet can give updates of the group's progress to the teacher so no child in the group can begin to 'tell tales' or 'steal the show.' Once the group is working well together the puppet can elect to choose a new leader, showing the children that it is only fair to take turns. As with many activities, it's amazing how using the puppet as part of the team also encourages children to verbalize what they are thinking. Children will explain to the puppet what the group is busy doing.

- **Merrily we go round:** Circle time activities can be used across any area of the curriculum when children need to listen and share their opinions and ideas. A small puppet can be passed round the circle and when each child is holding the puppet it's their time to talk. Shy children who are less confident at talking to the class can address their ideas to the puppet. Children should also be allowed to pass the puppet on without speaking if they really don't want to, and then at the end of the round, these children could be given another opportunity to share if they wish. Ask the children to shake the puppet's hand or give it a smile before passing it on, as this seems more positive than telling them to say 'pass.' When the puppet has gone all round the circle, the teacher can use the puppet to recap what the children have talked about.

Drama

Year 1 Learning objectives	Year 2 Learning objectives
Explore familiar themes and characters through improvisation and role-play	Adopt appropriate roles in small or large groups and consider alternative courses of action
Act out their own and well-known stories, using voices for characters	Present part of traditional stories, their own stories or work drawn from different parts of the curriculum for members of their own class
Discuss why they like a performance	Consider how mood and atmosphere are created in live or recorded performance

Puppet activities

- **Class logistics:** Drama can be approached in a whole range of ways to suit different classes and styles of teaching. Some classes may have several shy children who find it hard to relax and enjoy drama and need the process to be built up slowly with activities such as 'hot-seating' first. Other classes may be brimming with confident children who get carried away with the opportunity to act out the story and of playing in role – puppets can help give a considered and structured start to drama and involve everyone.

- **No costumes required:** When using a puppet, it is not always necessary for the children to dress up in costumes. While some children relish the experience, others find it embarrassing. Using a puppet who looks like the character encourages the children to think dramatically about stories and characters without awkwardness.

- **Little space required:** When space is limited finger puppets can be used to act out a story. Children can still engage with the characters, use appropriate voices and have an awareness of their audience. Small puppets also enable the children to be involved in making scenery or creating a setting for the story in an empty box or by using a large sheet of card in front of which the puppets perform.

Act out well-known stories with characters played by both children and puppets.

- **Audience appreciation:** Children need the opportunity to perform to an audience. By using puppets to play the characters, the children can take all the credit for any positive comments. Conversely in a story where the 'baddie' character might elicit a 'boo' or jeer, that interaction can be seen as directed towards the puppet and not the child.

- **Filming performances:** Digital technology has now made it possible for either pupils or the teacher to film their puppet performance using either the video mode on a digital camera or simple camcorder devices. An advantage of using puppets for the performance is that it can be shared immediately with a wider audience on the web without any images of the children being involved. Getting feedback on their performance from other groups of children and also watching other puppets perform is a wonderful motivator for the children and gives them a real sense of purpose for their work.

Word recognition

Children enjoy sharing books with puppets. Even before they are able to read the words, the child can to tell the puppet the story by using the pictures and the puppet is sure to react in exactly the way the child wants.

Children need to be taught letter sounds (phonics), CVC words and also high frequency irregular words such as 'the' and 'said'. Puppets can help to make this fun for children with imaginative activities and different games so that although the learning is repeated and reinforced , they don't become bored, disheartened or frustrated.

Puppets love being told your favourite story and sharing a book with a friend.

Year 1 Learning objectives	Year 2 Learning objectives
Recognise and use alternative ways of pronouncing the graphemes already taught	Read independently and with increasing fluency longer and less familiar texts
Recognise and use alternative ways of spelling the phonemes already taught	Spell with increasing accuracy and confidence, drawing on word recognition and knowledge of word structure and spelling patterns
Identify the constituent parts of two- and three-syllable words to support application of phonic knowledge and skills	Know how to tackle unfamiliar words which are not completely decodable
Recognise automatically an increasing number of familiar high frequency words	Read and spell less common alternative graphemes including trigraphs
Apply phonic knowledge and skills as the prime approach to reading and spelling unfamiliar words that are not completely decodable	Read high and medium frequency words independently and automatically
Read more challenging texts which can be decoded using their acquired phonic knowledge and skills, along with automatic recognition of high frequency words	
Read and spell phonically decodable two- and three-syllable words	

Puppet activities

- **I spy with my finger puppet:** Ask a child to identify a finger puppet and its initial sound. Can they hold the puppet and find something else that begins with that letter? For example 'I spy with my puppet penguin, something beginning with 'P' and it's a pen.' The puppet can then be passed to the next child who thinks of another word beginning with the same letter. For some children it might be appropriate to let them know that they can to repeat a word said by someone else. Other groups could be extended by asking them to add a new item each time to create a list.

- **Puppet and letter sound snap:** Each child in the circle can hold a different finger puppet. Try and find finger puppets for different letters of the alphabet such as alligator, bear, cat, dog, elephant, fish, etc. Place a set of letter cards in the middle of the circle and take turns to pick a card and say the letter sound. If the letter is the same initial sound as their puppet the child has to say snap and keep the card. If the card doesn't match them, say the letters sound and places the card back face down. This game also encourages thinking and memory skills. Extend the activity by swapping puppets with a friend and playing again.

- **Flash cards:** These can be made with a small piece of rough-sided Velcro attached to the back of them. Many puppets can hold up these cards for the children to read which makes phonics and word games more fun. The puppet can store the cards in its own special magic bag or box. Puppets can play about and get away with holding flash cards upside down – a useful fun game for reinforcing early letter recognition skills and emphasising that letters must be formed the correct way round.

- **Letter lines:** Children often find letters with ascenders and descenders confusing. A dog puppet can show the children the letter 'd' and then explain, 'it's like me — a round tummy at the front and then at the back my tail goes up because I'm having fun!' A persona puppet can help with the letter 'b' — 'I always hold my bat first and then I put my ball next to it. Look, my bat and ball make a 'b' shape!' The parrot can show the letter 'p' and then explain that a parrot likes to sit on a perch. When sitting on the perch the parrot's tail feathers go straight down, just like the stick on the letter 'p', and the parrot always wants to see what's going on, so he sits with his tail behind him and looks along the line to see what is happening next.

- **Digraph duos:** Two small puppets can be used to make up games when the children are learning about digraphs. Each puppet can have a letter and the children can look at the individual sounds. When the puppets hold hands something magical happens and the two sounds make one new sound!

Puppets can play literacy games.

- **Guess the word:** Attach cards to the puppet's hat or blindfold him and write the words on the board. Can the puppet guess what the word is? He can ask what the first letter is and then make some guesses, sensible or daft! If his guess is wrong he can ask for another clue. When the puppet has modelled the game, a child can take his place. The game can be made trickier if the children are only allowed to give 'yes' or 'no' answers.

  - **Letter swap:** The puppet can stick the letters 'l' 'e' and 'g' on to his hat and get the children to tell him the sound that each letter makes and the word they spell. He can then change the 'l' to a 'b' so the children sound out and read 'b e g' and make a new rhyming word. Then with the wave of a magic wand and the saying of the 'naughty **e** spell!', the puppet removes the 'g' and now the 'e' says 'ee'! Can the children read the word now — bee. This can lead on to a discussion about the words 'see' and 'sea' and then be extended to 'seen' and 'scene'. The possibilities are almost endless but great fun!

Word structure and spelling

Year 1 Learning objectives	Year 2 Learning objectives
Spell new words using phonics as the prime approach	Spell with increasing accuracy and confidence, drawing on word recognition and knowledge of word structure, and spelling patterns including common inflections and use of double letters
Segment sounds into their constituent phonemes in order to spell them correctly	
Recognise and use alternative ways of spelling the graphemes already taught	
Use knowledge of common inflections in spelling such as plurals, -ly, -er	Read and spell less common alternative graphemes including trigraphs
Read and spell phonically decodable two- and three-syllable words	

Puppet activities

- **Word games:** Unfortunately for the puppets and the children only half the key words they need to know are phonetic. Puppets can turn this unfortunate truth of the English language into a host of funny games. They can fill brightly-coloured boxes and bags with key word cards, or stick them on their t-shirts, coats and hats. A wide piece of smooth-sided Velcro attached to the puppets clothing and a selection of word cards with rough-sided Velcro on them, allows the puppet to play lots of hiding and guessing word games.

- **Magnetic fishing game:** The children sit in a circle and the area in the middle is the pond – a shiny piece of blue fabric would add to the setting of the scene, but isn't essential. A set of coloured fish have words or letters written on the reverse, a hole punched in them and a paper clip threaded through. At the start of the game, the puppet can hold the fishing rod – a short wooden stick with a magnet hanging from the end. He catches a fish and tells the children what's written on the back. If he's right he keeps the fish, if he's wrong it has to be thrown back into the pond, and the puppet passes the rod to a child to have a go. The role of the puppet in the game is to model the activity, keep the children actively engaged and of course add enjoyment.

Puppets can turn learning spellings into a game or quiz.

- **Puppet quiz:** The puppet can turn learning spellings into a game or quiz. He can give out clues for his spelling challenge, or hot tips for his next quiz. He rolls the tombola drum and pulls a ticket out with a magic word on it and asks the children to write on one of their tickets the same word he has found.

The learning potential of puppets can be increased by providing a good collection of props that can be used to engage the children in word level learning, such as boxes of objects that can be sorted by initial sounds, or items that the children can sort into rhyming groups.

The puppet can sing words and letters, paint them boldly, or write them in a fine shiny gel pen for the children to copy and learn. The puppet ensures that the children are actively engaged in their learning.

Sentence structure and punctuation

Year 1 Learning objectives	Year 2 Learning objectives
Compose and write simple sentences independently to communicate meaning	Write simple and compound sentences and begin to use subordination in relation to time and reason
Use capital letters and full stops when punctuating simple sentences	Compose sentences using tense consistently (present and past)
	Use question marks, and use commas to separate items in a list

Puppet activities

- **Word sort:** The puppet can pretend to be a little confused and end up with his words in a muddle! Or he can try out his new scissors and chop up some sentences so that they don't make sense. Children love to help out, and the puppet will be thrilled when they sort the words out for him!

- **Mind the gap:** Not only does the puppet get his words jumbled up but sometimes he leaves gaps in his writing if he's not sure what to write! The puppet can bring in a letter he has written to his mum with gaps where he can't remember when to use he, she, or they. The children can explain and then help him fill in the gaps.

- **Tense pretence:** The puppet can bring in a postcard from where he went at the weekend but he can't remember how to write in the past tense. He told the children what he was going to do on Friday, but now on Monday he's not sure how to write about what he did! The children can explain how to write a recount in the past tense. The puppet can read it back to make sure it makes sense and then shriek in delight that it's great.

- **Reality check:** Using a puppet also helps give relevance and meaning to activities. Children will be far more motivated to match captions to a series of photographs if they are shots of the puppet on holiday, or photos of themselves doing activities in the class that the puppet took with his own camera!

- **Punctuation exercises:** The puppet can teach the children actions to represent different punctuation marks such as, hands held up as a stop sign for a full stop, a slow gentle wave for a comma, and a salute for a capital letter. The puppet then reads the children a short extract and the children do the actions where they think the punctuation marks should go.

- **Commas in lists:** The puppet can show the children a tray of objects to remember and then hide them. Play Kim's game and ask the children to remember all the objects that they have seen. The puppet writes them across the board using no punctuation and then asks the children how they can make the words into a list with commas. When the children check the tray, if they find any objects that were forgotten, they have to explain how these items can be added to the list.

- **Making connections with connectives:** The puppet can help the children to make a word web using all the facts they know about him. Photocopy the word web and then cut the copy up so that each idea is on a separate piece of paper. Alternatively, make the word web on an interactive whiteboard, print it out and cut it up. The puppet can now play a game giving two children each an idea from the web for example: 'Tim has blue jeans. Tim has a red top.' They read out their ideas and then a child comes between them and suggests a connective that could join the two ideas together. 'Tim has blue jeans and a red top'. A variation can be played where the puppet has a list of different connectives and he can try placing them into sentences i.e. the children show him with a thumbs up or down if he has made a good choice.

Understanding and interpreting texts

Puppets can bring with them a favourite book to share with the children. A large persona puppet can sit on an adult's knee and help turn the pages and show the children that he is listening to the story attentively by watching the teacher. Smaller puppets can choose to sit on a child's knee to enjoy the story. A finger puppet on the teacher's finger can peep in and out of the book! The puppet can watch the children and whisper in the adult's ear the names of any children who are concentrating really hard. The children will be especially interested in the story when they know it's the puppet's favourite. He can encourage the children to bring in their favourite books to share. Puppets can be used as props for storytelling and can add some secret things that aren't written in the book. The puppet knows what happened next or what different characters are thinking, but can the children guess? Children can read a book or tell a story to their puppet and make the audience respond in a variety of ways.

Puppets can be used as props for storytelling.

Year 1 Learning objectives	Year 2 Learning objectives
Identify the main events and characters in stories, and find specific information in simple texts	Draw together ideas and information from across a whole text, using simple signposts in the text
Use syntax and context when reading for meaning	Give some reasons for why things happen or characters change
Make predictions showing an understanding of ideas, events and characters	Explain organisational features of texts, including alphabetical order, layout, diagrams, captions, hyperlinks and bullet points
Recognise the main elements that shape different texts	Use syntax and context to build their store of vocabulary when reading for meaning
Explain the effect of patterns of language and repeated words and phrases	Explore how particular words are used, including words and expressions with similar meanings

Puppet activities

- **Quiz time:** Children's comprehension of a story can be checked by the puppet taking on the role of quiz master. He can simply ask the children questions about the story directly, or he could write some questions on the board, read them with the children, and then give them time to talk to a partner and prepare answers. The puppet can then ask each pair to answer a question and the others to vote with thumbs up or down if they agree with the answer. A more extrovert puppet could even deliver his quiz in a 'Who wants to be a Millionaire?' format.

- **Tell me more:** If the puppet is a character from the story, he can ask the children questions that get them to think about what might have happened if... or what might happen next.

- **Hot seating:** Children can take turns in the 'hot seat' and take on the role of a character in the story. The puppet can show them how to interview or pose questions to the child. Hot seating is made more effective if props from the story are used as well. The puppet can demonstrate how to use the props.

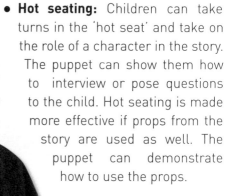

"Tell me more: Where did you get your hair done?!"

Engaging with and responding to texts

Year 1 Learning objectives	Year 2 Learning objectives
Select books for personal reading and give reasons for choices	Read whole books on their own, choosing and justifying selections
Visualise and comment on events, characters and ideas, making imaginative links to their own experiences	Engage with books through exploring and enacting interpretations
Distinguish fiction and non-fiction texts and the different purposes for reading them	Explain their reactions to texts, commenting on important aspects

Puppet activities

- **Read with me:** Set up a reading area with comfortable chairs, beanbags or large cushions, and put out a few puppets with their favorite books all ready to share them with a friend. Reading a book with a puppet is a good way for shy or less confident children to practise reading out loud. Children who cannot yet read all the words can use picture clues to tell the story to their puppet, and still enjoy the experience of sharing a story.

- **Story boxes and sacks:** These are available commercially, or can be made by putting a copy of a book, with relevant puppet/s or finger puppets, props, materials or pictures to help set the scene, into a box or bag. Let children work both individually or in small groups, reading the story and retelling it using the puppets and other items to recreate the setting and events in the story.

- **All types of text:** Puppets can help children get interested in a whole range of texts, fiction and non-fiction. The puppet can bring in cookery books, dictionaries and information books on a wide range of subjects including topics the children are doing, and any other subjects he thinks the children might be particularly interested in. He can show them the instructions for playing his new game, football magazines and articles in the local newspaper. He can bring in leaflets picked up at the doctors or supermarket on healthy eating. When a child in the class announces their family has got a new cat, the puppet can bring in a book on looking after pets.

- **Reading enthusiast:** The puppet can be a role-model of avid and enthusiastic reading for the children. While the puppet shares his love of reading, he also nurtures that enjoyment in the children. The puppet should have a card for the local library and can show the children some of the marvelous books he has borrowed. He can accompany the children on a visit to the library and encourage them to join.

Read with me!

Creating and shaping texts

'I must send a postcard back to school to tell them all about our fabulous holiday here in Cornwall.'

Puppets can provide children with lots of different opportunities for writing such as making cards for birthdays, Christmas or other festivals and writing letters to say 'get well soon' or 'thank you'. The puppets will want to reply, and the children can help them. A puppet can be placed at a writing desk, ready with writing implements, some fancy writing paper, or white board pens and a small board, waiting for children to come and join him. Children need to see a purpose for writing and using a puppet provides lots of reasons for writing. The children can help the puppet think of what he wants to write, and as they watch him write sentences on the board they can check that he has remembered the correct punctuation, putting their hands up if they spot any mistakes. The puppet can ask the children for help with words he gets stuck on and this can reinforce the learning strategies that children use to help them spell. He can ask a child to read back what he has written and ask the children for their opinion of his work. He can even ask them to think of ways to make his writing more interesting. Children will be keen to come up with good suggestions to help ensure that the puppet does an excellent piece of writing.

Children can be given puppets to play with that can hold a pencil, either birds with large beaks, or persona puppets who can hold the pen in their hands or mouth. This makes the experience of writing more fun for young children, and takes away the pressure of the writing being neat or even making sense as the child can say 'The puppet did it!', or of course if the writing is receiving praise, the child can say, 'I did it!', or 'I showed the puppet how to do it!' Puppets can own all sorts of fancy writing implements that they share with the children such as pink sparkly gel pens, thick florescent green markers, or those wonderful biros which change colour. Plain grey pencil is too dull for the puppet to use all the time!

Sometimes the puppet may not want to write the word, so he could also have access to letter cubes, so he can build the word, letter stamps and ink pads so he can stamp out the word, and even sponge and foam stencils so he can print out the words. Classroom puppets can use interactive whiteboards and have fun writing in programs like 2Simple 2Handwrite (www.2simpleshop.com), or using moving letter cards, or matching pictures to words. Try accessing the internet and use some of the many excellent sites with fun activities for letter and word recognition such as Words and Pictures (www.bbc.co.uk/schools).

Year 1 Learning objectives	Year 2 Learning objectives
Independently choose what to write about, plan and follow it through	Draw on knowledge and experience of texts in deciding and planning what and how to write
Use key features of narrative in their own writing	Sustain form in narrative, including use of person and time
Convey information and ideas in simple non-narrative forms	Maintain consistency in non-narrative, including purpose and tense
Find and use new and interesting words and phrases, including story language	Make adventurous word and language choices appropriate to the style and purpose of the text
Create short simple texts on paper and on screen that combine words with images (and sounds)	Select from different presentational features to suit particular writing purposes on paper and on screen

'Another wonderful day on our camping holiday for us to write up about in our diary tonight.'

Text structure and organisation

Year 1 Learning objectives	Year 2 Learning objectives
Write chronological and non-chronological texts using simple structures	Use planning to establish clear sections for writing
Group written sentences together in chunks of meaning or subject	Use appropriate language to make sections hang together

Puppet activities

- **Invitation writing:** All kinds of events can be organised which will require the children to help the puppet to write invitations. Children also relish the opportunity of inviting their parents and carers to join in with class activities, such as reading parties, big art days, super science days, class assemblies, presentations of stories they have been doing in literacy, and recounts of school trips.

- **Writing letters and cards:** Puppets provide many reasons for the children to write letters and cards. On his birthday the children will all want to send the puppet a birthday card. He may be sick and the children can send the puppet get well cards. In return the puppet can send the children a 'thank you' card to tell them how much better their cards made him feel!

- **Puppet postcards:** If the puppet goes away somewhere exciting, he can send the children a postcard telling them all about it. On his return he can bring something exciting to show them. The essential point is to demonstrate to the children the importance of writing and to give it relevance.

'Did I tell you the story about this magical dragon whose favourite colour was red? Once upon a time, the dragon met a boy wearing a red t-shirt ...'

- **Writing instructions and lists:** Once the invites for the puppet's party have been written and given out, he will need help organising the food and party games. Can the children write out some instructions for party games they enjoy? Ask the puppet to read out their instructions and see if the games work. The children can follow recipe instructions to make the puppet's favourite food. They will soon discover that if instructions are not written in the correct order, then the results are not what you want!

- **Recounts:** When any event is over, such as a school trip or special visitor to the school, the children can enjoy sharing the experience with others. If the puppet wasn't fortunate enough to join in the event, he can be a perfect audience for them to share with. A vital precursor to writing is the ability to talk about the subject you want to write about. Puppets give children the opportunity to practise recalling orally events in sequence. Then the children can put their thoughts in writing, again with a purpose, for they can share their writing with the puppet too.

- **Story writing:** Puppets can be used in many ways to help children learn about writing stories, but most importantly they should encourage children to find story writing fun. To motivate and encourage children to write stories that they are already familiar with, they can start by telling the story to a puppet who hasn't heard it before and then writing it down for him to read, with illustrations of course. Puppets can be used to help the children retell the story so that they are better able to sequence the events and put the story into sentences.

- **Original stories:** Making up a story and writing it down is a complex task for a young child to do. Using puppets helps teachers to differentiate the activity so that all the children can have a go. For some children making up a story and being able to tell it to an audience will be a significant achievement. The size of the audience may depend on the child's confidence and range, from telling it to a friendly puppet or an adult with some support, to a small group, and then to the whole class. Using props like puppets can help the child to structure the story in their mind before they write it down.

- **Improvising stories:** An excellent way to spark ideas for story writing is to provide children with a couple of small hand or finger puppets, a few props such as a bus ticket, a postcard, some shells, etc. The choice is endless. Through playing with the puppets and handling the props, children may come up with a story idea. Having been given the opportunity to have fun with the puppets, making up a story, acting it out in sequence and creating dialogue between characters, the children can be encouraged to write down their stories, either independently or with some support. If children feel that their story is going to be enjoyed by others, they should be encouraged to take their puppets and props, and share it with other children, adults or friends. The more children are encouraged to verbalise their ideas, the easier they will find it to write them down.

Presentation

Year 1 Learning objectives	Year 2 Learning objectives
Write most letters, correctly formed and orientated, using a comfortable and efficient pencil grip	Write legibly, using upper and lower case letters appropriately within words, and observing correct spacing within and between words
Write with spaces between words accurately	Form and use the four basic handwriting joins
Use the space bar and keyboard to type their name and simple texts	Wordprocess short narrative and non-narrative texts

Puppet activities

- **Write it:** A puppet with hands that can grip a pen can demonstrate how to form letters to children. As the puppet writes, the adult can describe the movement the pen is making. The children can join in by writing the letters in the air, on a partner's back with their finger or on small white boards. If the puppet gets it wrong, then a child can demonstrate to him how to do it right. The puppet can then try again, get it right, and be full of praise for the child who has helped him learn how to form the letter. He can remind the children that it was just a case of listening, watching and trying a few times.

- **Present it:** The latest Primary Curriculum Review encourages more use of ICT to present stories. Children can act out their stories using puppets and the performance can be filmed or photographs taken of the key scenes. Children can use the photographs to create illustrated books on the computer using programs such as Textease (www.softease.com) or software from 2Simple (www.2simpleshop.com). Watching their own story re-enacted on the interactive whiteboard or on the internet is very exciting and motivating. Encourage children to share their stories, with other classes in school or take copies home.

Teaching and learning mathematics with puppets

In order to develop skills in all areas of mathematics children have to acquire basic knowledge of mathematical concepts such as counting and understanding numbers, using number facts, recognising shapes, measuring, handling data and of course problem solving. This section looks at the different ways in which the puppets can make this journey relevant and exciting. It takes key learning objectives from the framework for mathematics and introduces ideas for teaching and learning with puppets.

Puppets help to ensure that maths lessons have elements that will engage all learners: visual, kinaesthetic and auditory. The puppet can bring number problems to life by setting up real situations with problems for the children to solve, e.g. sharing out his sweets or working out his change. The puppet won't always know the answer and sometimes will get things wrong allowing the children to see that it is acceptable to get things wrong and encouraging them to explain to the puppet their methods for finding the right answer.

My personal favourite puppet to use in mathematics lessons is 'Tim', a large persona boy puppet with hands and fingers that can be manipulated. Consequently, many activities are described as though using him, but they can be adapted for use with any size puppet if your budget won't stretch to this. Even a little finger puppet, will add interest and fun! Puppets that make a noise, such as a large bird that squawks can repeat its noise to signal a number, and a bird puppet can hide objects in its beak or hold a pen. Whatever puppet you choose, its use is greatly extended by the use of props that the children associate with the puppet. This can easily be achieved by placing the props in a special bag or box which 'belongs' to the puppet.

'2 + 8 = Squawk!'

Using and applying mathematics

When a teacher poses a mathematical problem to the class, some children will immediately think 'I can't do that' or 'I'm sure I'll get the answer wrong'. They will probably not even consider how they could solve the problem. They will be too busy thinking how they can avoid being asked the answer or wondering if now might be a good time to ask to go to the toilet! If the puppet poses the problem to the class, not only will the children be keen to help, but they will also want to make sure that the puppet understands the method they used. If another child knows a different strategy then they can share it too, without the first child feeling that their answer was not good enough. If the class is struggling to find any answers for the puppet, the teacher can make a suggestion such as 'I wonder if it would help us solve the puppet's problem if we tried the method ... remembered the fact that ...'

The important thing with problem solving is for children to get plenty of practise at applying solutions in different scenarios. When one problem is posed some children may not have been able to find the answer. They may need to listen to another child describe how they solved it and then the next time a similar question is posed they can apply this method. By using a puppet it's possible to do repeated problem solving without it becoming repetitive. The puppet will be full of praise and thanks for the children's help. It's also vital that children learn to explain how they got their answer. Using a puppet encourages this dialogue, as the children may feel that the teacher knows the strategies already but explaining how they did it to the puppet makes more sense.

Year 1 Learning objectives	Year 2 Learning objectives
Solve problems involving counting, adding, subtracting, doubling or halving in the context of numbers, measures or money, for example to 'pay' and 'give change'	Solve problems involving addition, subtraction, multiplication or division in contexts of numbers, measures or pounds and pence
Describe a puzzle or problem using numbers, practical materials and diagrams; use these to solve the problem and set the solution in the original context	Identify and record the information or calculation needed to solve a puzzle or problem; carry out the steps or calculations and check the solution in the context of the problem
Answer a question by selecting and using suitable equipment, and sorting information, shapes or objects; display results using tables and pictures	Follow a line of enquiry; answer questions by choosing and using suitable equipment and selecting, organising and presenting information in lists, tables and simple diagrams
Describe simple patterns and relationships involving numbers or shapes; decide whether examples satisfy given conditions	Describe patterns and relationships involving numbers or shapes, make predictions and test these with examples
Describe ways of solving puzzles and problems, explaining choices and decisions orally or using pictures	Present solutions to puzzles and problems in an organised way; explain decisions, methods and results in pictorial, spoken or written form, using mathematical language and number sentences

Puppets can help with problem solving.

Puppet activities

- **Making decisions:** Children are taught many different skills in mathematics, and they need to be able to decide which skill to use to solve each particular problem. The puppet can pose many questions during mathematics sessions and throughout the day to develop this ability, for instance when they are sharing fruit, milk or birthday sweets, taking the register or lining up. Which of the puppet's apples is the largest? How could the children prove it? Which piece of wrapping paper is big enough to wrap up this present? The puppet only has 10 grapes left in his fruit bowl. If he was going to give everyone in the class two grapes, how many would he need?

- **Shape sharing problems:** Use the puppet to encourage children to think about problems where more than one answer can be correct, and let the children explain their thinking process. You should ask:
  Which piece of paper could the puppet use to make a hat?
  Which shape would be best to use as a wheel on the puppet's model?
  Which shape would the puppet choose to make a sail on his boat?
  Can you design a picture of a house for the puppet using a large and a small triangle, square, rectangle and circle?

Sadia works out the answer to additions and subtractions by walking her puppet up and down her number line.

- **Think of a number:** Explain that the puppet is going to think of a number for the children to identify using some clues. Which number is the puppet thinking of if it is an even number, more than 40, less than 60, with 2 digits that add up to 8? Which number is he thinking of if it is more than 20, less than 25, and can be divided by 3 but not by 4?

- **Money matters:** If an apple costs 5p and a banana costs 8p how many apples and bananas could the puppet buy and not have any change left from £1?

  If the puppet gets 5p pocket money every week, how much will he get in a month?

  It is his birthday on the 10th of June and he gets a £1 from his mum, he also gets a £1 at Christmas time, so how much money does he get altogether?

- **Amazing puppets:** Guide the puppet out of a maze using the instructions, left, right and forward only.

The puppet is building a Lego house, with a garage and driveway and he wants to make sure he can park his car and his friend's car on the drive. How long does he need to make the driveway?

- **Pick a problem:** The puppet can write some of his questions down on paper and these can be used as extension activities or even as tasks for children to discuss before registration. Children can also be encouraged to write their own questions which the puppet can help them with, and then the puppet can ask the other children to help him.

Counting and understanding number

Puppets can be used in lots of different ways to develop counting skills with children of all ages. With younger children the number of objects can be relatively small and easier to handle, using the numbers 1 – 10. As the children progress the puppet can increase the number of items he is counting and can begin to use strategies such as tallying to help. Children can be asked to come up with solutions to help the puppet count larger numbers of objects and should be encouraged to make estimates too.

The puppet can demonstrate one to one correspondence by touching each item as he counts it. Sometimes he might carelessly count on one, but move on two objects, and the children who are watching and listening closely will have to correct him and explain to the puppet why he went wrong. Children can be encouraged to join in by demonstrating to the puppet what he needs to do to be an accurate counter.

Don't forget to let the puppet get the answer wrong sometimes! This shows the children that it's acceptable to get the answer wrong and the fundamental importance of the word 'yet'. The puppet doesn't know the answer... 'yet'. But with the children's help, he soon will!

Year 1 Learning objectives	Year 2 Learning objectives
Count reliably at least 20 objects, recognising that when rearranged the number of objects stays the same; estimate a number of objects that can be checked by counting	Read and write two-digit and three-digit numbers in figures and words; describe and extend number sequences and recognise odd and even numbers
Compare and order numbers, using the related vocabulary; use the equals (=) sign	Count up to 100 objects by grouping them and counting in tens, fives or twos; explain what each digit in a two-digit number represents, including numbers where 0 is a place holder; partition two-digit numbers in different ways, including into multiples of 10 and 1
Read and write numerals from 0 to 20, then beyond; use knowledge of place value to position these numbers on a number track and number line	Order two-digit numbers and position them on a number line; use the greater than (>) and less than (<) signs
Say the number that is 1 more or less than any given number, and 10 more or less for multiples of 10	Estimate a number of objects; round two-digit numbers to the nearest 10
Use the vocabulary of halves and quarters in context	Find one half, one quarter and three quarters of shapes and sets of objects

Puppet activities

- **Count me in:** At the beginning of a maths session, the puppet could be busy counting and the children will eagerly begin to count with him. He could be lining up his football cards and checking how many he has or just counting his fingers. He can drop his pocket money on the floor and pick up the coins, count them and check hasn't lost any.

- **Other items puppets like to count:**
  - Shells brought back from a day at the seaside.
  - Other natural objects, such as autumn leaves, pine cones and pebbles.
  - Biscuits in a packet. Sweets in a jar / bag. Has he enough to share!?
  - Grapes in a bunch. A healthy alternative to the one above.
  - Raisins in a box. Apples in a bowl. Lots more healthy options.
  - Children sitting quietly on the carpet. That's all the children once they realise who he is counting!
  - Display items on the whiteboard for him to sort and count.
  - He can count on from different numbers on a number square, count even or odd numbers or count backwards.
  - He can count along the numbers on a number line, or count as he jumps along a number line on the floor.
  - Toys cars in his collection. Puppets can have all sorts of collections, depending on what the children like, e.g. marbles, stickers, conkers, buttons, collectable coins, trading cards, lollipop sticks, plastic dinosaurs, snakes, fish, etc.
  - Use a picture, chart or illustrations to count objects, such as how many players in his favourite team, or how many different types of ice cream the local ice cream van sells.

- **Listen and count:** Try counting where the children cannot actually see the objects, e.g. the puppet can drop coins into a tin, clap his hands together or make sounds using a squeaky toy, drum, or other musical instrument. Children find this harder so begin by showing them a number, and then listen to see if the puppet can make that many bangs on his drum. If not a child will have to help him, by telling him how many more or less he needs to do, or even by demonstrating it for him!

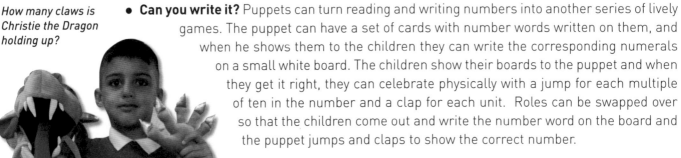

How many claws is Christie the Dragon holding up?

- **Can you write it?** Puppets can turn reading and writing numbers into another series of lively games. The puppet can have a set of cards with number words written on them, and when he shows them to the children they can write the corresponding numerals on a small white board. The children show their boards to the puppet and when they get it right, they can celebrate physically with a jump for each multiple of ten in the number and a clap for each unit. Roles can be swapped over so that the children come out and write the number word on the board and the puppet jumps and claps to show the correct number.

- **Flashing fingers:** Persona puppets can be a great resource for place value and ordering activities. Clench the puppet's fingers together and then open them again to show ten fingers. Repeat this three times, encouraging the children to count how many lots of ten the puppet is showing them – 30. Then show just a few fingers – four. The children have to say what number the puppet has shown or 'flashed' them – 34. Try another number. Encourage the children to explain their answer saying how many lots of ten the puppet showed them and how many units. This activity can be varied in many ways to keep it fresh or appropriate to children's needs. Children could suggest a number or write it on the whiteboard for the puppet to 'flash', or they could 'flash' a number using their own fingers for the puppet to work out.

- **In the right place:** Children can help the puppet sort larger numbers of articles into groups of tens and units. Can they count how many groups of 10 there are and then how many units? The puppet can write the number on the board for the children. Sometimes the puppet may reverse the digits and the children can explain to the puppet where he has gone wrong and how to correct the mistake.

- **Two-digit problems:** The puppet can show the children objects which show groups of ten, such as ten unifix cubes joined together or chocolate coated biscuits with ten sweets on top. The puppet can pose problems for the children to solve such as 'If I eat three whole biscuits and this piece with only three sweets left on it, how many sweets will I have eaten altogether?' Make the problems fun and the children are more likely to remember the methods they use to answer them.

- **Techno puppets:** Many computer programs can be used on an interactive whiteboard to demonstrate place value, and a puppet with moveable fingers is able to interact with the board just like the children. Try the National Strategies Interactive Teaching Program (www.nationalstrategies.standard.desf.gov.uk) on place value – an excellent tool to use with your puppet.

- **Computer games:** There are also lots of games on the internet designed to help children learn about numbers or practise the skills they have learned. If you are unsure where to start here are some websites to try — www.bbc.co.uk/schools , www.topmarks.co.uk , www.amblesideprimary.com. Children seem to love the games even more when they believe it's their class puppet's favourite. The practitioner can demonstrate the game, but by doing it with the puppet, you're not setting up the game as 'Beat the teacher' but rather 'Beat the puppet's score!', which makes it a lot more fun. You can make sure that the puppet gets a score that the children can realistically beat, while children expect their teacher to get a high score.

- **Keep in order:** Ordering numbers is an activity that puppets can adapt to numerous games. Number cards can be dropped by accident and the helpful puppet can try and get them back into order. The children will be keen to help and can tell the puppet how to do it too. 'Oh, dear, a couple of the cards seems to have got lost!'. Can the children help the puppet by finding out which cards are missing and then help to make new ones?

- **Roll up, roll up!** Number games can be made up by the puppets, based on those played at school fairs. Try 'Pick-a-straw' – roll up small pieces of paper with numbers on, or raffle tickets and slip them inside straws. The puppet can pick one out, open it and show a child his number. They can read the number for the puppet, who then can choose another child to come and pick a straw and find the number hidden in it. Try different versions of the game, e.g. the winner can be the child who gets the highest or lowest number, or the number nearest to a multiple of 10 or 5. Variations on the game can be made simply by hiding the numbers in different ways such as on a plastic duck in 'hook a duck' or on a plastic ball in a ball pit. Use dice to make number games – the puppet can roll two dice, one dice to show the number of tens, and one dice to show the number of units. Can the children work out the number for him?

- **Puppet milkman:** Our school milk is delivered in cartons wrapped in blocks of ten. Try washing out a few day's worth of cartons and repacking them in plastic so they look like the real thing but obviously are much lighter. The puppet and the children can have fun pretending to be milk men. How many cartons will they be able to deliver in one minute?

- **Guess the number!** Try some estimating and rounding activities. Children can sometimes be nervous about estimating as they are used to an answer needing to be correct, and guessing the number of objects can seem odd! The puppet, however, has no such fear of getting things wrong and will be happy to give an estimate. Sometimes the guess can be clearly wrong, e.g. the puppet can estimate 100 apples in a bag. The children can then explain why this isn't a sensible answer. Puppets show children that it's okay to get the answer wrong, and encourage children to have a go.

- **Keep guessing:** The more opportunities children are given to estimate numbers, the more accurate they will get. Each time the puppet brings a selection of objects into the class, the children can be asked to guess how many there are before they count them with the puppet. Try estimating the number of sweets or grapes in the puppet's bowl and the nearest estimate wins the food!

- **Round about:** The puppet can extend many number activities to give children practise in rounding numbers up to the nearest 10. He can use his fingers to flash a number indicating a number of tens and units, and the children can tell the puppet the number and then work out the number which is the nearest multiple of 10. Children can pick folded raffle tickets out of the puppet's tombola box and can 'win' if the number is a multiple of 10, or if they can tell the puppet what the nearest multiple of 10 would be.

Knowing and using number facts

Don't forget to let the puppet get the answer wrong sometimes!

The learning of all key facts requires lots of practice but it is crucial that children develop the ability to recall number facts quickly. Each time a child practises key number facts it is rather like running along a path through an overgrown field. At first it will take a long time, and sometimes they may get lost and give in, but each time it will get easier and the path will get clearer. So it is with messages passing through the brain; the more the children do it, the easier and faster those connections will be made. The danger with children and repetition is that they can get bored and switch off. This is where the beauty of using puppets comes in, as a puppet has the power to keep the learning lively and fun. With a little imagination, puppets can make every session on number facts or tables more enjoyable, with the children smiling and laughing as they interact with the puppets. Getting children to explain their answers to the puppet, or using the puppet to clarify how they got the answer is a brilliant way of reinforcing a child's learning and good for checking that they have understood the method.

Rapid mental recall of number facts

Persona puppets are brilliant quiz masters. They can be far more animated and exciting than even the most flamboyant teacher! The puppet turning over flash cards and firing the questions for 'Number bond Mastermind!' is so much more interesting than the teacher asking the questions. Sometimes the puppet can get it wrong and say 'The answer is 20! Whoops! I've told you the answer so we'll have to give the point to whoever can tell me the question!' Problem solving with all the children inspired and engaged then begins! A puppet working in a school with interactive whiteboards will enjoy engaging with the children in games like 'Table Mountain' (http://www.teachingtables.co.uk) or 'Number Bonds Machine' (www.amblesideprimary.co.uk). Children love to play at being teacher so let them take turns at testing the puppet too. How quickly can he answer their questions?

Year 1 Learning objectives	Year 2 Learning objectives
Derive and recall all pairs of numbers with a total of 10 and addition facts for totals to at least 5; work out the corresponding subtraction facts	Derive and recall all addition and subtraction facts for each number to at least 10, all pairs with totals to 20 and all pairs of multiples of 10 with totals up to 100
Count on or back in ones, twos, fives and tens and use this knowledge to derive the multiples of 2, 5 and 10 to the tenth multiple	Understand that halving is the inverse of doubling and derive and recall doubles of all numbers to 20, and the corresponding halves
Recall the doubles of all numbers to at least 10	Derive and recall multiplication facts for the 2, 5 and 10 times-tables and the related division facts; recognise multiples of 2, 5 and 10
	Use knowledge of number facts and operations to estimate and check answers to calculations

Puppet activities

- **Multiple counting:** As children start to learn to count in 2s, 5s and 10s, the persona puppet can keep the children motivated by making it fun. When counting in 2s, the puppet can bring in his bag of dirty socks for the children to count with him. Counting in 5s becomes more interesting when the puppet chooses some friends and they count how many fingers they have by using all their hands. The popularity of the cartoon character Ben Ten has done much to provide the puppet with a new and exciting way to learn the 10 times-table – how many Bens do you need to create 50 aliens?

- **Halve it!** When teaching fractions you will discover your persona puppet has a great liking for Battenberg cake! For anyone who has never come across this wonderful teaching tool, it is a cuboid-shaped cake held together with a covering of marzipan, and divided into four small squares of cake two pink and two yellow. A puppet with a Battenberg cake in its shopping bag will provide children with a memorable experience that should firmly implant the concept of halves and quarters into their brains! The puppet can cut slice after slice of the cake and get the children talking about how it can be shared in even halves and quarters.

- **Healthy fractions:** Children always love the combination of food and puppets, but the puppet can also teach fractions in healthier ways!

"My puppet can give me a hand. I'm adding five and counting on her fingers. I know we can work it out together!"

- The puppet can cut up apples to share them with a friend (halves) or with 3 other children (quarters).

- **Sandwich fractions:** The puppet can make sandwiches with the children and cut them into halves and then quarters. Then he can invite the children to come and take a quarter each. Can they cut the quarter sandwiches into triangles and make eighths?

- **Show me a shape:** The puppet can use a small whiteboard and ask the children to draw a shape, such as a square and then divide it into two by shading in one half. The puppet can then ask the children to show him their boards and the children can explain why there are different possibilities which can all be right. Repeat the game with a quarter, or invite a child to give the instructions. Can the puppet draw the shape and divide it into different fractions with the children deciding whether he has done it right or not!

- **Sharing fractions:** To explore number fractions with the children, the puppet can bring in many objects to share. The puppet can choose two or four children who have been working particularly well and say that he wants to share his last 8 stickers with them. The children can suggest ways that the puppet could work out how many stickers to give each child. He can practise with 8 cubes and then when he knows how to do it fairly, he can share out his stickers. The puppet can have all sorts of other things to share: grapes, raisins, conkers, even jokes written on slips of paper! 'I have six jokes to tell you but there's not time to tell them all today so I'll keep half of them for tomorrow!' How many jokes will the puppet tell the children today?'

- **Magic shapes:** The puppet can pretend to be a magician and tell the children that he can fold a square in half and change its shape. He can give the children time to try and solve the mystery, and if they can work it out they can come and perform the trick with him. Otherwise the puppet can wave his magic wand, ask the children to join in with the magic spell, and then fold the square piece of paper over to form two rectangles. The whole performance can be repeated to change the square into two triangles! The more spectacular and animated the show, the more the children will remember the experience and the learning associated with it.

- **Sharing problems:** The puppet can suggest relevant problems for the children to help him solve.

  - 'I have 20p pocket money and I want to buy a comic off my big brother. He says it costs half of my pocket money. How much will I have to give him and how much will I have left?' The learning can be extended by asking the children to explain why the two answers are the same.

  - 'My favourite football team has scored 10 goals this season. My dad says the best player has scored half of all those goals. How many goals has he scored?'

  - 'My mum wants my sister and I to eat 5 portions of fruit and vegetables a day each. How many portions does that mean we will eat altogether in one day?' The puppet can ask the

Calculating

Many of the suggested activities for using puppets to develop counting and number skills can be expanded to demonstrate calculation too. For instance, when the puppet has counted out all his toy cars he can realise that he has left two at home. Can the children work out how many cars he has altogether? The puppet can count out his pencils but then remember that three of them belong to the teacher or one of the children. Once he has given them back, how many pencils does he have left?

Year 1 Learning objectives	Year 2 Learning objectives
Relate addition to counting on; recognise that addition can be done in any order; use practical and informal written methods to support the addition of a one-digit number or a multiple of 10 to a one-digit or two digit number	Add or subtract mentally a one-digit number or a multiple of 10 to or from any two-digit number; use practical and informal written methods to add and subtract two-digit numbers
Understand subtraction as 'take away' and find a 'difference' by counting up; use practical and informal written methods to support the subtraction of a one-digit number from a one-digit or two-digit number and a multiple of 10 from a two-digit number	Understand that subtraction is the inverse of addition and vice versa; use this to derive and record related addition and subtraction number sentences
Solve practical problems that involve combining groups of 2, 5 or 10, or sharing into equal groups	Represent repeated addition and arrays as multiplication, and sharing and repeated subtraction (grouping) as division; use practical and informal written methods and related vocabulary to support multiplication and division, including calculations with remainders
Use the vocabulary related to addition and subtraction and symbols to describe and record addition and subtraction number sentences	Use the symbols +, −, ×, ÷ and = to record and interpret number sentences involving all four operations; calculate the value of an unknown in a number sentence (e.g. $* \div 2 = 6$, $30 - * = 24$)

Puppet activities

- **Playing dice games:** Persona puppets enjoy playing games with dice. Place a large snakes and ladders board in the middle of a circle of children. The puppet can help to demonstrate how to play the game using two dice, adding the numbers together and then moving that number of squares on the board. The activity can be extended for more able children by encouraging them to add the numbers on the dice to the number of the square the puppet is on and calculate where to move to. Can they compare the numbers at the top of the ladders to the number at the bottom and calculate how many squares they have moved on? Puppets can also play board games like this on the interactive whiteboard with the added benefit that all the children can see the screen clearly.

- **Magic tricks:** Puppets can perform lots of magic tricks – with the wave of a wand and a quick 'abracadabra' children are mesmerised and keen to watch what the puppet is about to do. He can show the class a number of small objects on a tray, and then cover them with a brightly coloured or sparkly cloth. After a suitable magical gesture such as waving his wand, saying a spell, or jumping up and down, he removes the cloth. 'Wow! Now there are * [insert different number] on the tray'. The children have to work out what calculation the puppet's magic trick has performed. A different number of objects are placed on the tray and the magic can be repeated over again. The children can say how many objects they think there will be on the tray now and explain their answers. The puppet then pulls the cloth away to reveal the answer. Of course if the puppet has done a different spell this time, then a different calculation will have been performed. It helps to protect the magic if the children close their eyes during the spell and that way they won't see you put your hand under the cloth and change the number of objects!

- **Missing numbers:** Persona puppets with fingers can write down simple calculations, hide them from the children, and then tell them part of what they have written down to see if the children can work out the missing numbers. For example, the puppet could say 'I have written 4 + * = 10' . The children can write down the calculation with the missing number and show it to the puppet, or the puppet can choose a child to say the answer. The game can then be played with a child taking the role of scribe and the puppet having to guess the whole calculation that has been written down.

- **More missing numbers:** Extending the activity to using 3 numbers in an addition calculation provides the children with the opportunity to realise that sometimes more than one answer can be correct. For example, the puppet can give the children a calculation such as 5 + * + * = 15. They can generate lots of different answers that could be right, so the puppet can add another clue, such as the missing 2 numbers are different and both odd numbers. This would narrow the options down to 5 + 1 + 9 = 15, 5 + 9 + 1 = 15, 5 + 7 + 3 = 15 or 5 + 3 + 7 = 15, all of which are right. Problem solving, when a puppet is setting the problem is much more engaging. The puppet can appear very surprised that the children keep coming up with different answers, which although they may not be what he has written down are correct calculations. He is leading the children in the direction of that 'eureka' moment! Puppets can celebrate that with far more style, panache and enthusiasm than most teachers could get away with!

- **Up and down the line:** Puppets can help demonstrate the use of a number line in addition and subtraction calculations most effectively. They can lay out a large number line on the floor and then start at a given number and jump up or down the appropriate number of spaces. They can push cars, roll marbles, or small balls, set off wind-up toys, all from given places on the line and then help the children work out how many places up or down the item has moved.

- **Threading beads:** The persona puppet can make his own jewellery by threading beads. This involves all sorts of calculations. 'I've threaded on 6 red beads so far but I would like to have 10 red beads on my necklace. How many more do I need?' This sort of questioning can be extended as follows: 'Oh dear! I think my friend would prefer a pattern of 5 red and 5 blue beads instead of the 10 beads all being red. How many red beads do I have to take off now?' These are practical problems which the children can see and interact with. It can then be written down to show the calculation, either by the teacher, a pupil or the puppet.

- **Multiplying beads:** This can also lead the puppet into multiplication and division problems. 'I need 20 beads on my necklace and I can use 4 different colours, how many beads do I need in each colour?' 'Now! The necklace needs to be longer so if I add one more bead of each colour how many beads long will it be?' The children can work out the answers and explain how they did it to the puppet. This type of questioning works so much better when you use a puppet because when the teacher asks how they worked it out, a child can think 'you already know how, because you told me!'

- **Money, money, money!** Puppets love using money and so do children! Nothing makes numeracy seem more important or more relevant than handling coins. When teaching addition the puppet can have a coin in one pocket and then find another coin they had forgotten about in the other pocket. 'Oh look! I've got 5p in this pocket and in my coat pocket I've got a 10p coin. How much have I got altogether?' The puppet can extend the question – 'I had 20p pocket money this week, how much have I spent?' All this problem solving is consolidated when the children explain their answers and then write down the calculations. Try using notes for the puppet to count by printing Monopoly money from the Internet for free!

Puppets can help demonstrate the use of a number line.

- **Multiplying money:** The puppet can use money to demonstrate multiplication by dropping coins into his money box. He can drop five 2p coins into the tin and ask the children to work out how much he's putting in altogether. As he drops in each coin he can count and write 2+2, and then 2+2+2, and so on until 2+2+2+2+2 is written on the board. The children can work out the answer 10. 'How many lots of 2 did we add altogether?' asks the puppet and when the children reply 5, he can write 5 x 2 = 10 on the board to show how the calculation can be written down.

- **Food, glorious food!** In addition to money, the puppet's other favourite subject is food! 'I only have 20 biscuits but there are 30 of us! How many more biscuits do I need to get so we can all have one?' 'I have 4 bars of chocolate and each has 5 pieces. How many pieces of chocolate do I have altogether?' 'I had 10 sweets in my packet to start with, but I've eaten 3, so how many are left now?'

- **Five a day!** Healthy alternatives can also be used for calculations, such as grapes, strawberries, and raisins for numbers over 20, while lower numbers can be counted with larger pieces of fruit. The introduction of the National fruit scheme means that most classes up to year 2, will have a piece of fruit for each child in the class. The puppet can make excellent use of this to demonstrate different calculations . The fruit arrives packed in bags of ten, so the puppet can easily set up lots of simple addition and subtraction problems and can also show the connection between the two operations. 'Oh dear! This bag of apples is open, I hope none have fallen out. Let's count them to see how many are left in the bag'. The puppet and children count 8 apples. The children work out that 2 are missing, and the calculation 8 = 10 - 2 is written on the board. The children can then calculate how many apples to add to the 8 to make the bag back up to 10 again.

Understanding shape

Children learning about shape will soon become a captivated audience as the persona puppet performs what will appear like a series of tricks and magic acts for them.

Year 1 Learning objectives	Year 2 Learning objectives
Visualise and name common 2-D shapes and 3-D solids and describe their features; use them to make patterns, pictures and models	Visualise common 2-D shapes and 3-D solids; identify shapes from pictures of them in different positions and orientations; sort, make and describe shapes, referring to their properties
Identify objects that turn about a point (e.g. scissors) or about a line (e.g. a door); recognise and make whole, half and quarter turns	Identify reflective symmetry in patterns and 2-D shapes and draw lines of symmetry in shapes
Visualise and use everyday language to describe the position of objects and direction and distance when moving them, for example when placing or moving objects on a game board	Follow and give instructions involving position, direction and movement
	Recognise and use whole, half and quarter turns, both clockwise and anticlockwise; know that a right angle represents a quarter turn

See if you can spot the cuboids and cylinders in our building.

Puppet activities

- **Guess the shape:** In a glittery magic bag, the puppet can hide some shapes, plastic 2–D shapes, or better still his treats for tea time: a wagon wheel biscuit, a piece of Toblerone, a healthy bar, and a square slice of bread! The puppet can only give the children yes or no answers and they have to guess the shape of the things in his bag, and then what they might be.

- **3–D shape sorter:** Similar games can be played with 3–D shapes and the puppet can hide a box of raisins, a can of pop, an ice cream cone, and a chocolate orange in his box! Or try some healthy options – a tube of tennis balls, a rubix cube, a book, and a party hat!

- **Fruit shape salad:** The puppet can help children to create a fruit salad which is a medley of all the 3–D shapes they know. Use a melon baller to create spheres. Cut cubes out of apples or pears. Cones are trickier to create but with a bit of imagination you might be able to transform the tip of a banana or a carrot!

Puppets can help children learn on the computer.

- **Folding shapes:** The puppet can perform great acts of magic, and with the wave of his wand, and the chanting of a spell, he can turn a square of shiny paper into a triangle, or a rectangle, or a cone shape! The children can then go onto recreate the magic too.

- **Model shapes:** Matchsticks and blu tack or plasticine, or the tastier version – marshmallows and cocktail sticks or spaghetti, can all help the puppet show 2–D shapes such as a squares, triangles and rectangles. Can he help the children create 3–D shape models?

- **Symmetrical paintings:** Puppets and children will revel in the magic of symmetry. The puppet can show the children how to create wonderful butterfly paintings simply by folding a piece of paper in half, daubing paint on one side, then folding the paper over and pressing down. When the puppet slowly opens the paper he can gasp in delight as he sees a perfect symmetrical butterfly emerge!

- **ICT symmetry:** The puppet can use 2Simple 2Paint (www.2simpleshop.com) on the interactive whiteboard to create symmetrical pictures really easily. The children can watch the other half of the picture taking shape while the puppet or a child draws on one half of the screen.

Measuring

The persona puppet can engage the children in lots of practical activities to help them understand and use the vocabulary related to length, mass and capacity. The puppet can also become obsessed with telling the time, sporting a whole range of his own smart watches, alarm clocks and timers!

Year 1 Learning objectives	Year 2 Learning objectives
Estimate, measure, weigh and compare objects, choosing and using suitable uniform non-standard or standard units and measuring instruments (e.g. a lever balance, metre stick or measuring jug)	Estimate, compare and measure lengths, weights and capacities, choosing and using standard units (m, cm, kg, litre) and suitable measuring instruments
Use vocabulary related to time; order days of the week and months; read the time to the hour and half hour	Read the numbered divisions on a scale, and interpret the divisions between them (e.g. on a scale from 0 to 25 with intervals of 1 shown but only the divisions 0, 5, 10, 15 and 20 numbered); use a ruler to draw and measure lines to the nearest centimetre
	Use units of time (seconds, minutes, hours, days) and know the relationships between them; read the time to the quarter hour; identify time intervals, including those that cross the hour

Puppet activities

- **What's the measure of it?** The puppet may have noticed that the children in the class all seem to be taller than him. Who does he think is the tallest in the class? What could they use to measure height? Children can explore measuring themselves using uniform non-standard units such as straws, cubes, etc., and then can progress to using centimetres and metres, guided by the puppet.

- **Weights and scales:** Having investigated heights, the puppet can now find out about different weights. Can they use the same or different units to measure with? Will the tallest child also be the heaviest?

- **Measuring items:** The puppet can bring in a very interesting collection of items for the children to measure. They can discuss the different weights and sizes of a peacock feather, a straw, a long nail, and a stone. The children have to place them in order of length. Is the longest item also the heaviest, and the smallest the lightest? First of all, the children can hold the items and estimate their weights before placing them in weight order. How can they check their results?

- **Water, water, everywhere!** Capacity and puppets always leads to some hilarity, especially with the aid of a water tray! The puppet can get the children to fill all sorts of containers and find out which holds the most water. The advantage of using the puppet is that he can invent scenarios that give a purpose to the children's investigations. He can plan to go on a picnic with some friends so he needs to make sure that he chooses a container big enough to hold at least one cup of juice for each of them.

- **What's the time Mr Puppet?** The puppet can show off his range of very interesting watches and even an alarm clock which he tries to set to tell the class when it's time for lunch. But he doesn't know how to use the watches and clocks properly and asks the children to help him. Just to make it trickier, the puppet wears an analogue watch one day, and a digital watch the next, and then he'll need lots of help because he can't find any big or little hand on it!

- **Alarming sounds:** Can the puppet set several alarms so that they go off with different sounds for instance, a mobile phone, an alarm clock, radio alarm clock, a wind-up egg timer and a sport's watch. Set the alarms to go off at key times in the school day such as playtime, lunchtime, etc. At the end of the day, can they recall which alarm went off at morning play, or when did the mobile phone alarm clock go off? Can they remember the order in which the alarms sounded?

- **Time travel:** Having introduced the children to lots of different alarms, play games where the children have to make their own alarm sound, or vibrate (shake!) when the class clock shows a certain time. The puppet can notice that it's nearly 10.30am and time for play, and shake while making a wondrous beeping sound as soon as he sees the minute hand reach the 6!

Capacity and puppets always leads to some hilarity, especially with the aid of a water tray!

Handling data

Year 1 Learning objectives	Year 2 Learning objectives
Answer a question by recording information in lists and tables; present outcomes using practical resources, pictures, block graphs or pictograms	Answer a question by collecting and recording data in lists and tables; represent the data as block graphs or pictograms to show results; use ICT to organise and present data
Use diagrams to sort objects into groups according to a given criterion; suggest a different criterion for grouping the same objects	Use lists, tables and diagrams to sort objects; explain choices using appropriate language, including 'not'

Puppet activities:

- **Organising and using data:** The puppet can play a game using dice. He takes it in turns to roll the dice with the children. The winner is the person who rolls the most sixes, but he keeps losing count. What can be done to help?

- **Favourite fruit facts:** The puppet wants to find out which fruit the children in the class like best. He can ask the children which is their favourite fruit but he can't remember how many like each different fruit? Can the children help him to keep tally and then create a pictogram to show the results?

"I am playing a dice game with my puppet. We take turns to roll the dice."

Tips, techniques and resources

Tips and techniques

The whole ethos of using a puppet is about adding a little magic to the classroom environment, creating a positive learning state and enhancing enjoyment. Your decision to buy a puppet, or to begin to use one that has been tucked out of sight in a cupboard for a while, should not add to your stress as a teacher! Often when teachers are given a 'new tool' to help them, it comes with a training session or a manual – not so your puppet. I have heard some people talk about taking the puppet home and practising in front of a mirror to build up their confidence. That wouldn't be my way, but if you feel it would work for you – try it. My advice would be to just jump right in and start using the puppet with the children – you then have the best audience and critics in the world. They won't expect their teacher to be an expert ventriloquist or a budding dramatist – they will be on your side. If you are convinced it will add fun to the lesson and help the children learn, then that is exactly what will happen.

Some boys can be funny about relating to girl puppets so use a boy puppet to begin with.

- **Using a boy puppet:** If I was to get a puppet for the first time, I would definitely choose a boy persona puppet. Some boys can be funny about relating to girl puppets. They see the girl puppet as a doll and view it as a 'girlie' thing. I once had a long conversation with a boy, who when asked to sort pictures of toys into girls/boys/both put the dolls in the girl's section and Action Man in the boys. When I asked him about it, he was adamant that Action Man was not a doll – 'it's a person', he said. I showed him a picture of Ken and Barbie – Barbie was a doll, but Ken was still a person, he told me! Having started with a boy puppet you can go on to introduce all kinds of female persona puppets as friends and relatives of the original boy. Throughout this book we have referred to puppets as 'he' for ease of reference.

- **Naming:** Give him a name that makes you smile, and if possible is easy for the children to say and spell. My best mates have been Ben and Tim!

- **Grand entrance!** Make a big thing of introducing your new puppet to the children. I tend to arrange for the office to bring him down to the class at a specified time, and explain that he has just arrived at school and has asked to come and join our class! Particularly if you are using a persona puppet, it doesn't seem right to produce him out of a box or a cupboard – I prefer him to be brought in by someone. Alternatively, if you feel the office may doubt your sanity, you can place the puppet in the classroom after playtime and tell the children that he was sitting outside the office waiting to join them.

This puppet has gone on a field trip to a nearby farm.

- **Why am I here?** Why has the puppet come into your class – give him a purpose! If you are starting a new topic, give the puppet a badge, bag or box with props related to the topic. If you intend the puppet to be part of your maths or literacy lessons, tell the children that he has come to learn with them.

- **Time out!** When the puppet isn't being used in a lesson, it's important that he maintains his dignity. I have a place where the puppet can sit and the children understand that he is just quietly watching what is going on. Sometimes I choose to put the puppet away, making sure that my cupboard door is never left open in case the children catch sight of him tossed on to a crammed shelf of books! If you choose to let the children 'play' with the puppet, establish some rules, so that they take good care of him.

- **I need a break:** I think that the persona puppet can be most effectively used, if not over used. Like anything else with children, too much of a good thing can become boring or certainly less exciting. Send the puppet off for a well-earned break, or let him catch a bug. He will return refreshed and the children will have so much to share with him about what they have been learning. Absence does make the heart grow fonder.

- **Work it:** Some persona puppets allow you to place your arms into the sleeves of the puppet and then their hands fit on to yours like gloves. They may also have a place to put your hand inside to access the puppet's mouth. As you only have two arms, you need to decide whether you are going to control the puppet's mouth and maybe one arm, or sit him on your knee and work both of his hands. Your choice will be based largely on what you want the puppet to do. I tend to operate both the arms of my puppet as I like him to be able to pick things up, point and clap. I don't usually make my puppet move his mouth as if he is talking. If I want to convey a message from the puppet, I pretend that he has whispered something to me by holding his head very close to my ear, and using my own facial expressions to provide clues to what he is telling me. You only need to hold the puppet next to your ear, raise your eyebrows and glance in one child's direction, and all the children will guess that the puppet was saying something about that child! The children will be watching your face and waiting to hear if it was good or bad news. If you choose to work the puppet's mouth with your hand, the children will most likely be watching the puppet and not your lips. Remember that they want the puppet to be alive and if you make no attempt to hide the fact that it is actually you talking, there should be no reason for them to point it out. You can hold your children's interest without a puppet. With a puppet, you will definitely have their full attention, so relax and enjoy the fun!

- **One smart comment:** You may feel anxious about a child spoiling the 'magic' created by the puppet. I can remember a child that I knew would have a go at doing this. He shouted out 'it's not real! I know it's not real – it's a puppet, and you're making it work!'. I had predicted that a child might say all this – he was so eager to get it out and so I let him. I acknowledged his comments with, ' That's correct, I'm giving him a hand!' and then turned my eyes to the other children and carried on. 'Shall we all give him a hand?' I asked, and with smiles on their faces and everyone engaged, on we went. The boy needed to be acknowledged, but then I was able to carry on, and within minutes he was also eagerly watching the puppet. You will know if you have a child who is likely to behave in this way, and you will react in just the same way as you would to any other outburst. Acknowledge it, deal with it, keep control and move on.

More tips on using puppets

- **Big is best?** Big puppets are definitely eye catching and memorable. How comfortable or confident you feel about using puppets has a lot to do with how much you personally like your puppets. I have a wonderful huge monkey puppet that I save to use when I am taking assembly because he's big enough to be seen by all the children. The logistics of handling a huge monkey in the smaller space of the classroom carpet area makes it cumbersome and awkward to manage. So I also have a smaller monkey glove puppet, and this is the one that I would use in the classroom. Sometimes the children comment on the fact that they have seen me with a bigger monkey, and I tell them that this is his son! Sometimes if I have used the monkey puppet on the carpet, when the children go off to do activities, I may give the teaching assistant a monkey finger puppet to use with her group.

- **Hold them high:** With all types of communication, eye contact plays a key part. Hold your puppet high enough so that when you are communicating with him, the children can see that you are looking at the puppet's eyes and he is looking back at you. When the puppet says something to the teacher, just a glance in the direction of a piece of work, object, display or even child, will communicate to the children exactly what they have been whispering about.

- **What's my identity?** Sometimes it can be good to elaborate further on the puppet's family history. By giving the puppet a birth certificate, establish a birthday date which can be planned for and a place of birth which the children can find out about. He can have parents and family that the children can ask about. The puppet can have his own life, even a passport to show the countries he has visited!

Puppets have families and pets too!

- **How am I feeling?** If we ask a child how they know if someone is feeling happy or sad they will describe the shape of the person's mouth – turned up or down. A puppet can illustrate that actually the whole position of the head and its movements provides us with lots of signals about how people are feeling.

- Quick glances back and forth express concern.

- Double takes back and forth express surprise.

- Not using eye contact is also very telling – if you ask the puppet something using his name and he looks at the ceiling or away, it is obvious that he's trying to ignore you.

- Stiff head and fixed eyes in the opposite direction express anger and rejection.

- Slow glances back to you then away again express embarrassment or hurt.

- Dropping head expresses sadness and slow movements express depression or sleepiness.

- Head up straight expresses stubbornness.

- Head to one side expresses anger or confusion.

- Looking from one child to another when the children are talking, implies the puppet knows what they are talking about.

- Looking from a child to a grown up who has a behaviour chart on her knee, implies that the puppet has seen something. If it's a reward chart he's spotted someone who needs rewarding, but if it's a consequence chart, it could be bad news!

Puppets need cuddles too!

Making puppets

There are whole books dedicated to the craft of making puppets, so I am only mentioning here those which I have personally used and found successful.

It is possible to change most soft toys into puppets by simply unpicking some of the stitching and removing the stuffing so that you can put your hand inside. (One word of caution - if sharing these puppets with children, make sure that there are no sharp bits inside the toy, for instance behind the eyes). Alternatively, add loops onto the limbs or back of the toy, so that you can manipulate the toy's movements. Items such as oven gloves, bath mitts, and hot-water bottle covers are sometimes made in the shape of an animal or doll, and all these can be changed into puppets.

Making puppets with children

- **Lollipop stick puppets:** Children simply use paper, fabric, or funky foam to make a character or animal and then attach it to a lollipop stick. In my own class, the children all made puppets to represent themselves. We used a sizzix cutting machine to cut out people shapes which the children then coloured and attached to lollipop sticks. At circle time, they all introduced their puppets to the class. Later in the year we cut out car shapes and added these to the lollipop sticks so it looked like our puppets were going off on a journey.

- **Wooden spoon puppets:** With the increased awareness of going 'green', try using recycled materials to make different puppets. Wooden spoons are fantastic for making simple people puppets, as the spoon itself is a light beige skin tone and the wood can be drawn and stuck on to easily. We added industrial sewing thread cones to the spoons, obtained, from a scrap recycling merchant to make fabulous character puppets for acting out the story of 'Cinderella'. It would also be possible to simply stick clothing to the spoon handle and use the puppet in a similar way to the lollipop stick puppets.

- **Rubber glove finger puppets:** Fabulous, yet so simple! These puppets are made by cutting out funky foam or felt shapes, and sticking on small pompoms, wobbly eyes and pipe cleaners for legs and arms. Cut the fingers off rubber gloves and then glue these on to the back of the foam shapes. This final part, I did for the children so I could use a stronger glue. Felt tips can also be used on funky foam to add decoration. In addition to these being great fun as finger puppets, the children can put the puppets on their pencils when they were writing about their characters, and write with them! This really seems to inspire the more reluctant writers and I have observed several children carrying on conversations with their puppets while busy writing about them!

- **Fancy finger puppets:** This idea is similar to the previous one but instead of rubber gloves use colourful knitted, fancy black or lacy gloves to make the base for the finger puppets and decorate them accordingly.

- **Mitten muppets:** Try using different types of mittens to make glove or hand puppets. Add noses, ears and eyes, or hair, horns and hats to create different characters.

- **Sock puppets:** A sock makes an ideal starting point for a puppet with a moving mouth as you can easily put your hand inside a sock and then tuck the end of the foot back between your thumb and forefinger to make the mouth move. I have used this basic start for making minibeast puppets, adding pipe cleaners and felt to make wings, legs, and antennae, etc.

Making and collecting resources

Make or collect an interesting and exciting range of props to use with your puppet and you will be able to use him across the curriculum to engage the children in learning in a fun and interactive way.

Key points to remember when making resources to use with puppets.

✓ Make sure that the resources belong to the puppet and he is happy to share them with the children.

✓ Try and build up a selection of resources that can be used to help children learn in all their learning styles.

✓ Keep it fun — let the puppet introduce the activities as favourite games and magic tricks.

Resources for literacy

● **Phonic flash cards:** Make sets of flash cards with each letter illustrated with a suitable word, for instance 'l – lion'. Stick double-sided sticky tape or velcro on to the back of the cards with the rough edge outwards, and then most of your puppets will be able to hold the card up. Use cheap carpet runners or carpet mats as boards and attach the flash cards on to them. The children can play with the cards and mats on the floor or with the carpet boards suspended on an easel or fastened to the wall or door.

Eyes bright with joy and a happy smile... Puppets bring fun to a childs learning experience

● **Name cards:** Make a set of alphabet cards using upper case letters and the children's names, plus photographs of the children. Also include pictures of the puppets you have in the class. For more unusual letters try using adults in school, or characters that the children know – X for X-men is a useful one to remember!

● **Action cards:** Make a set of alphabet cards which show actions rather than nouns. Take pictures of the children and the puppets performing different actions, cut out images from sport's papers, or use the internet, for example 'b for bounce', 'c for catch', 'd for dance', 'f for fly', etc. All kinds of games can be played where the puppet or the child mimes the action and the children have to guess the associated letter sound. Or show the letter and the children have to act out the answer.

● **Phonic books:** Having gathered together all the pictures and words you need to make your flash cards, also compile them into small books so that the children can access them independently.

● **PowerPoint phonics:** Make a PowerPoint presentation or Smart board notebook using pictures and letters. Add sound effects between each slide in the PowerPoint such as a round of applause or children laughing! However you decide to put together your alphabet, be it a book, slide show or interactive note book, make sure that your puppet is seen as the owner of the resource. Make a front page that says 'Tim's alphabet' or 'Phil's phonics'.

- **What's in the box?** Find an attractive box or cover a shoe box with pretty fabric or wrapping paper. Collect small objects so that you have one for each letter of the alphabet, and put them in the box with a set of alphabet cards. The puppet can play all sorts of games with the children. With younger children, he can have a different box or bag made up each week with just one letter and a selection of objects that begin with that letter. Add in an 'odd one out', i.e. one object that doesn't start with the letter and see if the children can spot it. For more unusual letters, play the game the other way round, with the puppet telling the children that only one object in the bag begins with the letter. The puppet can also play other games with the sets of objects, such as 'Kim's game', i.e. showing a selection of things to the children and then removing one and seeing if the children can work out which is missing.

- **Shaped cards:** Make sets of shaped cards that can be used in all kinds of games, such as flowers, fishes, cars or something connected with the class topic. Instead of building a word wall with brick shapes, children will enjoy making a flower bed, filling the fish tank, or creating a traffic jam, etc. with the letters and words they have learnt. The classroom will look much more attractive with these records of learning!

- **Hats!** Puppets love hats! Attach smooth velcro to the puppet's hat and the children can play lots of games using phonics. Stick a letter on his hat and let him guess which letter it is while the children give him clues. Make hats for the children to wear by cutting strips of card and attaching velcro to either end so that the hat can be adjusted to fit any child and also opened up and stored flat. The puppet can wear a hat with a vowel on it and the children can see if they can find a friend and then join with the puppet and make a CVC word. The puppet will be able to think of lots of phonics games the class can play and the children will probably come up with some ideas of their own too.

What has the puppet found in the box?

Resources for maths

Many of the resources suggested for teaching literacy with puppets can also be adapted to help teach maths, e.g. sets of cards, hats, PowerPoint shows, etc. Always refer to any flash cards as the puppet's cards, and try to use illustrations that the children will relate to such as pictures of themselves.

- **Number cards:** If you have an animal puppet create a set of cards which relate to the animal, such as lily pads for the frog or bones for the dog. By using different shaped number cards the children will feel that the game really does belong to the puppet. The same set of cards can be used for all sorts of activities, and even presented as an interactive wall display. A set of number cards from 1 - 10 can be used to help children learn number recognition, sort numbers into order, spot the missing number, find pairs of cards that make number bonds to 10, and lots of other games that the puppet can make up.

- **Counting collections:** Puppets need to make collections of things that the children can enjoy counting. Store different objects in a fancy bag or box (see 'What's in the box' above), and then as soon as the puppet shows the children the container they will immediately want to know what's inside it this time. Remember that as all children are born kinaesthetic learners, and that boys change learning styles later, it's a good idea to have collections of items that will interest the boys especially, such as snakes, dinosaurs, cars, football figures, etc. The girls will already be interested by the puppet and what he is playing with, but the boys will benefit from also being keen to get their hands on the objects being counted or sorted.

- **Painting by numbers:** Puppets also need collections of objects with numbers on them. Toy cars often come with numbers painted on the roof, or you can paint on numbers using bright nail varnish or enamel paint. Figures of footballers are also ideal as they come with numbers on their back. You can play games such as sorting them into order, or picking out the ones that have so many tens or units, or into teams of odd and even. To make the games more fun, give the puppet a football shirt with a number on, or make a set of numbers with rough velcro on the back to stick on his shirt.

- **Magic egg boxes:** Most supermarkets now sell eggs in boxes of ten, as well as dozens and half dozens. Decorate some of these and turn them into magical egg boxes that the children can fill with eggs made from modelling clay or salt dough. A bird puppet can play lots of games with the children guessing how many eggs are in the box. Let a child peep in and say if the guess was right, or higher, or lower, and the game can continue till they guess the correct number. Or the bird can show how many eggs are in the box and the children have to tell it how many more it needs to lay to fill the box. Depending on the model of bird puppet you are using and the size of eggs, you may be able to hold some in your hand inside the puppet and let them drop out so it looks like the puppet is laying eggs.

- **Collecting containers:** Collect all kinds of containers that your puppet could use for playing games. Try to collect similar containers in different sizes, i.e. fizzy drinks are available in different-sized plastic bottles. Children can use these kinds of props for games to help find out about capacity and measuring. The puppet likes a particular drink. Will he have more if he drinks two small bottles or one large bottle?

Storing puppets and props

The idea of creating props for your puppet to use is a great way to make the pupils' learning experiences even more fun and exciting. But all these wonderful items that you have made need to be stored away out of sight, or they lose some of their initial impact. However, they also need to be somewhere in your classroom where you can get to them quickly, such as in a cupboard. Then if the children appear to be struggling with a particular concept you can quickly think of a helpful game or prop and the puppet can dash into the cupboard and produce the necessary resources. Primary classroom cupboards are often very small and the shelves may be crammed with files and paper work, so I use plastic vegetable racks and place them under the shelves. Try using separate racks for literacy, maths and other games. The literacy games can be sorted into different sections: phonics, cvc words, keywords, sentence building, and then boxes for stories. Maths games can be sorted into sections for up to 10, up to 20, up to 100 including work on tens and units, shapes, and measures. Behind the door I have a series of hooks and the bags with collections of objects to count and story bags are hung up there.

Puppets should not be left out in the classroom unattended! Don't let your children see them slumped lifeless in the corner somewhere. I have one large persona puppet who joins in with lots of lessons and he has a small chair next to mine. A converted jewellery stand helps him sit up straight in his seat and then he is there ready any time I need him. All the other puppets are kept in the cupboard, either hung in labelled storage bags, or placed with the games I usually use them with. The cupboard door is kept firmly shut so they remain hidden until it's their time to come out and join in the fun.

The exception to this rule is in the Foundation stage where a few puppets should be placed in various areas so that children can play with them independently throughout the day. However in these circumstances it is important that the children know that the expectation is that they will treat the puppets with care and respect. If children are poking the puppets, playing with them roughly or just leaving them on the floor, remove them from all the play areas, talk to the children, and encourage them to come and ask if they would like a puppet to play with in an area.

Puppets are an excellent resource for all teachers to use, but buying a range of puppets can prove expensive so it's a good idea to share them between classes. The large persona puppets could be allocated to a class or year group, and stay with that class predominantly, although other teachers may invite him to visit children that used to play with him so he can see how well they are doing. Keeping puppets in a central area doesn't really work as they tend to get forgotten about, or else taken to a class and left in the cupboard. To assist practitioners with sharing resources and puppets, it's a good idea to have a staff meeting occasionally where practitioners are invited to bring along the puppets they have in their cupboard, and show them to the other staff, sharing ideas about how they use them.

Using photographs of puppets

Excellent teaching and learning resources can be made by using photographs of the puppets in different places or scenarios. Take your puppet out and about with you out of school. People may look at you a little strangely as you get your puppet to pose on the swing or in front of a building, but just remember the thrill it will give the children. Often I find that people come and ask what I am doing and when I tell them, I seem to change in their estimation from a raving lunatic to an extraordinary teacher or somewhere in between!

I recommend using a digital camera as you can do much more with the image, and also you can reproduce it immediately. I usually use Photoshop Elements for working with my pictures, but there are many other packages on the market which will all do an excellent job. Digital cameras now come in a vast range of capabilities and prices. Within this book it is impossible to provide a comprehensive guide to digital photography so here are some basic ideas and tips for getting started.

"Oh dear! The paparazzi are here again! We've been caught on our holidays and not at school!"

Puppets can suddenly be anywhere in the world!

- If you can't take your puppet with you to photograph, take another picture of the puppet and then using a digital imaging program select the puppet, copy it, and then paste it into a picture of the scene you have chosen. With a little bit of practice your puppet can suddenly be anywhere in the world, doing amazing feats, such as winning medals, scoring goals, riding a camel or taking part in a space mission! Similarly you can take pictures of the children, select, copy and paste them into a picture of your puppet on his holiday.

- Get your puppet to stand tall or sit up for a photograph. All sorts of things can be used to go inside your puppet instead of your arm. Try kitchen paper rolls or holders, rolling pins, or I use converted stands from days when I used to make costume jewellery. Coat hangers can be bent into various shapes to help pose puppets with moveable arms. Use double-sided sticky tape or velcro to help the puppet hide its eyes and count to 10 while playing hide and seek, or hold hands with another puppet. Remember too, that if the method you use can be seen on the picture, a little bit of cloning in Photoshop will get rid of the stand, or conceal any tape.

- Having created the photos you wish to show the children, you can either print them out, or show them on a computer slide show. Use an interactive whiteboard if available as the pictures are clear and large. They can be made into a series of screens in programs like Smart Notebook, and then the children can help add captions on the screen using interactive pens.

- PowerPoint presentations are another excellent way to show a series of pictures. Set them up as a continuous show, with animation and sound added between each slide. Add the puppet as a separate image on to a background picture, so he can also be animated and the children can watch him move across the screen.

- Pictures of puppets can be made into books for the children to enjoy. They can help decide which words should be written on each page, so that they are the authors of their own book about the puppet. Practitioners can select text from books to enhance an area the children are learning about or to reproduce a favourite story. Children will enjoy using a set of puppet books in small groups for guided reading. If possible, allow them to take the book home to share with their family, for even if they are unsure of all the words, they know the puppet character well and will be keen to share the book with others.

Puppets can be made into books for the children to enjoy.

- If you are going on a school trip with your class, introduce the destination to the children, by taking the puppet there first when you do your risk assessment and taking a series of photographs of him. It gives you the opportunity to show the children in advance some of the things they are going to see. The puppet can bring back a guide book that the children can look at as well. I took our class puppet, Tim to the National Railway Museum at York, and the staff there made him very welcome and even let him go and stand on Stevenson's Rocket to have his photograph taken. Seeing Tim on this train ensured that all the children knew which train was the 'Rocket' when they went on the trip. Tim came back with a badge from the museum pinned on his sweat shirt, and a guide book and map. I scanned in the map, so we could all see it on the interactive whiteboard and were able to trace Tim's steps around the museum.

Puppets visit many interesting places.

- Sometimes we get the opportunity to visit places during our holidays which we know the children in our class would love to see, but far more exciting than their teacher telling them about it, is the puppet bringing in snapshots and guide books. My puppets have sets of photographic books from their visits to Chester Zoo, and yearly holidays in Cornwall, where they are seen rolling up their trousers, building sandcastles, going deep sea fishing and even posing with champion surfers! Don't worry about appearing foolish, get your puppet ready to visit lots of different places or failing that, cut and paste them into some great scenes. Gradually you can build up a selection of little books about the class puppet which will bring reading alive for the children in your class.

How many lessons does it take to become a champion?

References and further reading

References

[1] Unicef *'Return to Happiness'* – http://www.unicef.org/infobycountry/grenada_23364.html

[2] Gordon Stokes. (1984) 'One Brain: Dyslexic learning correction and brain integration.' Three in One Concepts.

[3] Anne D. Forester and Margaret Reinhard. (1993) 'The Learner's Way' Peguis.

[4] Gardener's multiple intelligences outlined in Mike Hughes. (2001) 'Strategies for Closing the Learning Gap' Network Educational Press Ltd.

[5] Eric Jensen. (2008) 'Super Teaching'. Corwin Press.

Further reading

- Sue Palmer. (2006) Toxic Childhood. How the modern world is damaging our children and what we can do about it. Orion books.

- Jennie Lindon. (2005) Understanding Child Development. Linking theory and practice.

- Margaret Donaldson. (1986) Children's Minds. Harper Collins.

- Linda Pound (2005) How Children Learn. From Montessori to Vygotsky — Educational Theories and approaches. Step Forward Publishing Ltd.

- Geoff Petty. (2004) Teaching Today. A Practical Guide. Nelson Thornes.

- Robert Winston. (2003) The human mind and how to make the most of it. Bantam press.

- Robert Winston (2004) What Makes Me Me? Dorling Kindersley.

- Dr Tessa Livingston. (2008) Child of Our Time: Early Learning. Bantam Press.

- Dr Tessa Livingston. (2008) Child of Our Time: How to achieve the best for your child from conception to 5 years. Bantam Press.

- Ian Gilbert. (2002) Essential Motivation in the classroom. Routledge Falmer.

- Mike Hughes. (2002) Tweak to Transform. Network Education press.

- Daniel Goleman. (1996) Emotional Intellingence. Bloomsbury.

- S.J. Stein & H.E.Book (2000) The EQ Edge. Emotional Intelligence and Your Success. Stoddart.

- G. Dryden & J. Vos. (2001) The Learning Revolution. Visions of Education Series. Network Educational Press.

- Brandon Bays. (2003) The Journey for Kids. Thorsons.

- Rhonda Byrne. (2006) The Secret. Atria Books.

- Tony Buzan. (2003) Brain Child. Thorsons.

- Carla Hannaford. (1995) Smart Moves: Why Learning is Not All in Your Head. Great Ocean Publishers.

Some of these books were read more for personal interest, but they have given me ideas or knowledge that I have used within the book.

Websites

www.super-school.co.uk – my website.
www.tes.co.uk – read the primary and PSHCE forums.
www.bandapilot.org – website for SEAL.